2 CORINTHIANS

Power in

Weakness

A Guided Discovery for Groups and Individuals

Kevin Perrotta

LOYOLAPRESS.

CHICAGO

LOYOLAPRESS.

3441 N. ASHLAND AVENUE
CHICAGO, ILLINOIS 60657
(800) 621-1008
WWW.LOYOLABOOKS.ORG

Nihil Obstat	*Imprimatur*
Reverend John G. Lodge, S.S.L., S.T.D.	Reverend John F. Canary, D.Min.
Censor Deputatus	Vicar General
April 14, 2006	Archdiocese of Chicago
	April 18, 2006

The *Nihil Obstat* and *Imprimatur* are official declarations that a book is free of doctrinal and moral error. No implication is contained therein that those who have granted the *Nihil Obstat* and *Imprimatur* agree with the content, opinions, or statements expressed. Nor do they assume any legal responsibility associated with publication.

Unless otherwise noted, the Scripture quotations contained herein are from the New Revised Standard Version Bible: Catholic Edition, copyright © 1993 and 1989 by the Division of Christian Education of the National Council of the Churches of Christ in the U.S.A. Used by permission. All rights reserved. Subheadings in Scripture quotations have been added by Kevin Perrotta.

For Karol

Interior design by Kay Hartmann/Communique Design
Illustration by Anni Betts

ISBN-13: 978-0-8294-2326-6
ISBN-10: 0-8294-2326-5
Printed in the United States of America
06 07 08 09 10 Bang 10 9 8 7 6 5 4 3 2 1

Contents

How to Use This Guide

Y ou might compare the Bible to a national park. The park is so large that you could spend months, even years, getting to know it. But a brief visit, if carefully planned, can be enjoyable and worthwhile. In a few hours you can drive through the park and pull over at a handful of sites. At each stop you can get out of the car, take a short trail through the woods, listen to the wind blowing through the trees, get a feel for the place.

In this book, we will read excerpts from Paul's letter called 2 Corinthians. Because the excerpts are short, we will be able to take a leisurely walk through them, thinking carefully about what we are reading and what Paul's words mean for our lives today.

This guide provides everything you need to explore 2 Corinthians in six discussions—or to do a six-part exploration on your own. The introduction on page 6 will prepare you to get the most out of your reading. The weekly sections provide explanations that will help illuminate the meanings of the readings for your life. Equally important, each section supplies questions that will launch your group into fruitful discussion, helping you to both investigate Paul's letter for yourself and learn from one another. If you're using the book by yourself, the questions will spur your personal reflection.

Each discussion is meant to be a *guided discovery*.

Guided. None of us is equipped to read the Bible without help. We read the Bible *for* ourselves but not *by* ourselves. Scripture was written to be understood and applied in the community of faith. So each week you'll find background and explanations in "A Guide to the Reading," which draws on the work of both modern biblical scholars and Christian writers of the past. The guide will help you grasp the meanings of the readings. Think of it as a friendly park ranger who points out noteworthy details and explains what you're looking at so you can appreciate things for yourself.

Discovery. The purpose is for *you* to interact with 2 Corinthians. "Questions for Careful Reading" is a tool to help you dig into the text and examine it carefully. "Questions for Application" will help you consider what these words mean for your life here and now. Each week concludes with an "Approach to Prayer" section that helps you respond to God's word. Supplementary "Living Tradition" and "Saints in the Making" sections offer the thoughts and experiences of Christians past and present. By showing what Paul's words have meant to others, these sections will help you consider what they mean for you.

How long are the discussion sessions? We've assumed you will have about an hour and a half when you get together. If you have less time, you'll find that most of the elements can be shortened somewhat.

Is homework necessary? You will get the most out of your discussions if you read the weekly material and prepare answers to the questions in advance of each meeting. If participants are not able to prepare, have someone read the "Guide to the Reading" sections aloud to the group at the points where they appear.

What about leadership? If you happen to have a world-class biblical scholar in your group, by all means ask him or her to lead the discussions. In the absence of any professional Scripture scholars, or even accomplished amateur biblical scholars, you can still have a first-class Bible discussion. Choose two or three people to take turns as facilitators, and have everyone read "Suggestions for Bible Discussion Groups" (page 84) before beginning.

Does everyone need a guide? a Bible? Everyone in the group will need his or her own copy of this book. It contains all the portions of 2 Corinthians discussed in the weekly sessions, so a Bible is not absolutely necessary—but each participant will find it useful to have one. You should have at least one Bible on hand for your discussions. (See page 88 for recommendations.)

How do we get started? Before you begin, take a look at the suggestions for Bible discussion groups (page 84) or individuals (page 87).

When I Am Weak, Then I Am Strong

I must admit that our family dog is not very well trained. Sometimes he comes when called. Other times, he responds to cries of "Rupert, Rupert!" with a backward glance over his shoulder as he trots out of the yard and off to who knows where. So we are thinking of setting up an electronic fence. Unobtrusive transmitters will be placed along the property line, and Rupert will have to wear a special collar. Whenever he begins to step out of bounds, an electronic signal will activate a buzzer in the collar, reminding him where he belongs. The system will mark out a comfort zone for him—our yard—surrounded by a zone of discomfort.

In a way, Rupert reminds me of myself. I have a comfort zone too—a range of circumstances and activities where life seems good and I'm confident that I can handle whatever comes at me. Beyond that range lie difficulties, stress, and pain. As I edge up to the limits of my comfort zone, I begin to feel twinges of anxiety. Probably the same is true for many other people.

What happens if we cross the boundary and leave our comfort zone? Unpleasant sensations may get worse. There's a world of harsh realities out there. Nevertheless, getting an education, earning a living, raising children, making a contribution to society—every path in life leads outward to challenges and hardships, stresses and distresses. Often we have to step outside the range where we feel comfortable. Only then are we able to grow and mature. Yet, while challenges and hardships help us grow, they also reveal our shortcomings and limitations.

Even if we're inclined to take refuge inside our comfort zone, things happen that wreck our comfort. We fall victim to an accident. We get sick. We grow old. Feelings of safety and control ebb. Our weaknesses are exposed.

The apostle Paul was not a man to hole up inside his comfort zone. He spent a lifetime journeying outward from one hard situation to another. His goal was not to keep himself safe and secure but to make God's love known to people—to spread the news of Jesus of Nazareth. Pursuing this goal brought Paul face-to-face with problems that perplexed him, even discouraged him. Sometimes he ran out of material resources. He was jailed, beaten, and thrown out of town. Day after day, he felt his weaknesses—and in the process he made an immensely important discovery: our weaknesses are precisely where we encounter the power of God.

Paul mentioned his discovery in several of his letters. But he gave it special emphasis in the letter we are about to read—2 Corinthians. In this guide, we are going to read portions of the letter in an effort to understand Paul's discovery of the interplay between divine power and human weakness—and attempt to learn how to cooperate with God's power when we find ourselves far outside our comfort zone.

Paul seems to have made his discovery about God's power in human weakness in at least three stages.

Early in his life, growing up as a Jew, Paul learned from the Old Testament Scriptures that God resists the proud and shows kindness to the humble (Psalm 18:27). In the Old Testament, God often displays his power when people are at the end of their rope and call on him for help.

But the intersection of divine power and human weakness came into sharper focus in Paul's mind when Jesus revealed himself to him (see Acts 9:1–19). At this moment, Paul recognized that Jesus is the Messiah and Lord of all. But how had the Messiah and Lord acted on behalf of human beings? It was by enduring crucifixion—one of the most agonizing experiences of human weakness imaginable. Jesus played his part in God's purposes for humanity by submitting his human weakness to his Father, placing his fear and pain in God's hands (Mark 14:36; Hebrews 5:7). Through Jesus' obedient offering of his weakness and suffering to God, God reversed the effects of our disobedience to God: he broke sin's hold on us and granted us forgiveness and reconciliation (Acts 10:39–43). By the ultimate weakness of dying, Jesus conquered death. By rising from the dead, he became the source of God's life for us here and now, and the source of our ultimate resurrection into God's kingdom (1 Corinthians 15:20–28). Looking at Jesus, Paul realized—undoubtedly with utter astonishment—that God's power had become fully effective in human weakness.

Even after this amazing revelation burst upon him, Paul needed to discover its personal meaning for him. Paul did not write an autobiography, and neither his letters nor Acts of the Apostles (which provides accounts of his missionary work) give us enough material to write a full-scale biography. We cannot trace the step-by-step development of his thinking. But in 2 Corinthians, we can see that the reality of God's power in Paul's weaknesses dawned on him gradually. Paul learned about God's power in weakness as he tramped and sailed from city to city—far outside his comfort zone. He painfully experienced his own weaknesses and, at the same time, witnessed God's power at work.

In his letter, Paul shows us that he did not find it easy to take hold of the revelation of God's power in human weakness through Christ. In this, he is like most of us. We are both attracted and dismayed at the idea that God works in human weakness. The assurance that God wishes to be powerfully present in our lives is certainly welcome news. But we would rather that he did not make our weaknesses the sphere where his power becomes effective. We naturally prefer prosperity to poverty, abundance to need, health and wholeness to sickness and disability. God would meet our preferences if he chose to work mainly through human strength and well-being—if he acted in our lives mainly by preserving us from our weaknesses and from the dangers that threaten us and by keeping us prosperous, successful, vigorous, and young. That is to say, we would like it if God would reverse the human condition, rather than working through it. By accepting death on a cross, however, Jesus fixed his presence at the dark center of human weakness and suffering. He demonstrated God's commitment to act in and through our limitations, vulnerability to pain, and mortality. If we find this divine strategy hard to accept, we may be consoled by the evidence that Paul, too, found it a difficult truth.

At the heart of Paul's ability to live with the mystery of divine power in human weakness was his sense of a personal relationship with Jesus. Paul did not regard Jesus' acceptance of his weakness and his offering of suffering to the Father merely as a model—an example "out there" for imitation. Paul did, certainly, regard Jesus as a model (for example, see Philippians 2:1–11). But he viewed Jesus as a unique model, who enables us to imitate him by drawing us into his life. Jesus invites us to be united with him, by faith, and to undergo death and resurrection in him (Romans 6:1–11). In this way, we can join our weaknesses and sufferings to his while sharing in his submission of weakness and suffering to the Father. God's power at work in Jesus' weakness and suffering then becomes active in ours. Paul knew himself to be "in Christ" and knew Christ to be in him. Only in this way did Paul find the power to go forward through difficulties with trust in God, regarding his weaknesses as opportunities for God's power to be at work.

Although Paul says a great deal in 2 Corinthians about power in weakness, that is not the focus of his letter. Mainly, he is dealing with problems that have arisen in his relationship with the Christians in Corinth. Consequently, we have a manifold challenge in reading his letter. First, in order to understand what he is saying, we need to get a basic understanding of the situation he faced in Corinth. Second, we need to sift his letter for what it says about our theme—God's power in human weakness. Third, we need to consider what this message means for our own lives. Each week, the Guide to the Reading and Questions for Application will help you meet these challenges. Before we begin, it will be useful to take a brief look at the background to the situation in Corinth as Paul wrote.

To be honest, at a distance of almost two thousand years, it is impossible to say for sure what was going on in Corinth when Paul wrote 2 Corinthians. Our knowledge—which comes largely from Paul's two surviving letters to that community, 1 and 2 Corinthians—is sketchy. Here, however, is a plausible reconstruction of the situation.

Paul was the first person to preach the gospel of Jesus Christ to people in the city of Corinth, in central Greece, around the year fifty (Acts 18:1–18). The church community he established there was probably quite small. Apparently the whole community could meet in a single house—the home of Gaius (Romans 16:23), who must have been a moderately wealthy man. Archaeologists estimate that the home of such a person in Corinth at the time might accommodate fifty visitors. Thus everyone in the church in Corinth would have known Paul personally. Keep this in mind as you read Paul's letter and observe the stresses and strains in their relationship with him.

After staying for "a considerable time" in Corinth (Acts 18:18), Paul moved to Ephesus, roughly a couple hundred miles east across the Aegean Sea, in present-day Turkey. From Ephesus, Paul sent the Corinthians some letters. The first (see 1 Corinthians 5:9) has been lost. The second was preserved; it is now called 1 Corinthians (around AD 53–54).

Paul planned, after writing 1 Corinthians, to visit Macedonia, a region in northern Greece. He told the Corinthians he would travel to and from Macedonia via Corinth. As it turned out, he made only the first part of this double visit. Apparently, when he stopped in Corinth on his way to Macedonia, a painful incident occurred. Perhaps another Christian missionary, visiting Corinth at the time, criticized Paul before the church community, and the Corinthians seemed to agree with the criticism by failing to speak up in Paul's defense. Distressed, Paul left Corinth and continued on to Macedonia. From there, he decided to skip the promised return visit to Corinth and went back to Ephesus directly.

He then sent the Corinthians a sorrowful letter, no longer extant, calling them to reestablish their relationship with him (see 2:3–9—in this book, biblical citations refer to 2 Corinthians unless otherwise specified). Afterward, Paul received a report, perhaps from his assistant Timothy, that the Corinthian believers were open to a reconciliation; yet they felt hurt by his failure to carry through on his promise of a second visit. Paul's cancellation of the visit even prompted some in the community to question Paul's love for them. The Corinthians, we might think, were a bit supersensitive—a thought that may have crossed Paul's mind also. In any case, he wrote another letter (2 Corinthians), to resolve the remaining problems. Judging from the first part of the letter, the tensions between Paul and the Corinthians seem to be on the way to resolution.

A murky issue regarding the situation in the Corinthian church is the presence of outsiders who seem to be challenging Paul's leadership. Apparently, when the Corinthians began to have doubts and suspicions about Paul's authenticity and motives, some people who had come to Corinth from elsewhere tried to take advantage of these areas of vulnerability in Paul's relationship with the Corinthians (see 2:5). Perhaps these outsiders were Christian missionaries who wanted the Corinthian Christians to repudiate Paul and accept them as their pastoral leaders. They seem to have criticized Paul's preaching and presented themselves as superior to him. Some of Paul's remarks suggest that these outsiders were promoting an understanding of Jesus that Paul finds inadequate (4:2; 11:4). But while scholars have expended a lot of effort trying to figure out who these shadowing figures were and how their preaching diverged from Paul's, no conclusion has been reached.

You may have noticed that I specified that the problems between Paul and the Corinthians seemed to be moving toward resolution in "the first part of the letter." A puzzling feature of 2 Corinthians is that later in the letter, the problems seem to be worse than ever. Beginning in chapter 10, Paul suddenly changes his tone. He seems more upset than before. He feels backed into saying inflammatory things that he would rather not say. It seems that the hoped-for reconciliation with the Corinthians has fallen through (11:3–4). While in the first part of the letter there were hints that intruders in Corinth were causing problems, Paul left these intruders in the background (for example, 2:5). But now, in chapters 10 to 13, he speaks about them directly. The Corinthians seem to support and accept outsiders (11:20).

How can this sudden shift be explained? Scholars speculate that before adding chapters 10 to 13 to the letter, Paul received disturbing news from Corinth. Or perhaps these are part of a subsequent letter by him that was later combined with the earlier one. In either case, the apparent deterioration in the Corinthians' relationship with Paul demonstrates that Paul experienced not only the weakness of being persecuted by strangers who rejected the gospel but also the weakness of being misunderstood and rejected by believers who knew him well.

Some modern readers think of Paul as a mighty teacher who occasionally hurled rhetorical thunderbolts down on his opponents. There is some truth to that impression, as we will see, especially in 2 Corinthians 10 to 13. But the letter as a whole shows us a very human apostle who experiences suffering in many forms, yet goes on with his mission for Jesus.

Partners in Pain

Questions to Begin

15 minutes
Use a question or two to get warmed up for the reading.

1   What cheers you up when you're down? Is there a remedy for sadness that works for other people but doesn't work for you?

2   When was the last time you made a phone call or sent a letter or e-mail to give someone encouragement? Did it work?

Opening the Bible

5 minutes
Read the passage aloud. Let individuals take turns reading
paragraphs.

What's Happening

Paul writes to the Christians in Corinth to shore up his relationship with them. Rather than beginning with a discussion of problems that have arisen, he leads off with a prayer that reminds them of the common ground they share with him—their life together in Jesus Christ. Yet even in this prayer, Paul touches on a crucial area of misunderstanding between the Corinthians and himself. Some of them have begun to doubt his authenticity as an apostle because he often seems weak: he is battered by all kinds of hardships and persecutions. "Is all his suffering a sign that Paul is not truly spiritual?" they wonder. In his introductory prayer, Paul begins to show them a connection between suffering and genuine spirituality.

Paul speaks about Jesus' sufferings, his own sufferings, and those of the Corinthians. We know about Jesus' sufferings from the Gospels. We don't know what afflictions of his own Paul refers to here (perhaps he was more endangered than St. Luke lets on in Acts 19:21–41). We also don't know what problems the Corinthians were experiencing. But for an idea of the hardships that Christians faced in this period, see Hebrews 10:32–34; 1 Peter 4:12–16.

Paul has a cowriter of the letter, a member of his missionary team named Timothy (1:1). But when Paul writes "we," he often means "I." He sends his letter to Christians in Corinth and in "Achaia"—the province of which Corinth is the capital (1:1). He addresses them as "saints" (1:1), not to imply that they are already models of holiness but that that is what they should become.

The Reading: 2 Corinthians 1:1–11

God, the Source of Peace . . .

1:1 Paul, an apostle of Christ Jesus by the will of God, and Timothy our brother,

To the church of God that is in Corinth, including all the saints throughout Achaia:

2 Grace to you and peace from God our Father and the Lord Jesus Christ.

. . . the Source of Encouragement . . .

3 Blessed be the God and Father of our Lord Jesus Christ, the Father of mercies and the God of all consolation, 4 who consoles us in all our affliction, so that we may be able to console those who are in any affliction with the consolation with which we ourselves are consoled by God.

5 For just as the sufferings of Christ are abundant for us, so also our consolation is abundant through Christ. 6 If we are being afflicted, it is for your consolation and salvation; if we are being consoled, it is for your consolation, which you experience when you patiently endure the same sufferings that we are also suffering. 7 Our hope for you is unshaken; for we know that as you share in our sufferings, so also you share in our consolation.

. . . the Source of Help

8 We do not want you to be unaware, brothers and sisters, of the affliction we experienced in Asia; for we were so utterly, unbearably crushed that we despaired of life itself. 9 Indeed, we felt that we had received the sentence of death so that we would rely not on ourselves but on God who raises the dead. 10 He who rescued us from so deadly a peril will continue to rescue us; on him we have set our hope that he will rescue us again, 11 as you also join in helping us by your prayers, so that many will give thanks on our behalf for the blessing granted us through the prayers of many.

10 minutes
Choose questions according to your interest and time.

1 Paul refers to blessing in 1:3. We usually think of a blessing as a prayer that channels God's approval and grace to someone or something—like the prayer in 1:2. Is that the kind of blessing that is going on in verses 3–4? Who is being blessed? What word might describe 1:3–4?

2 Count up the occurrences of "console" and "consolation" and of various words for suffering. What conclusion do you draw from your findings?

3 Reread verse 9. Do you think Paul did not trust God before the experience he mentions here?

4 Paul doesn't give details of his recent suffering (1:8–10). What might account for this omission?

A Guide to the Reading

If participants have not read this section already, read it aloud. Otherwise go on to "Questions for Application."

1:3–7. Paul speaks from recent experience (1:8–10) about God as the source of help in the midst of hardships and difficulties (1:3–4). Paul does not envision a distant God "away up" in heaven sending help to us "down here" on earth. At the center of Paul's picture of God's relationship with those who suffer is God's Son, who did not remain in heaven but came to be with us as a human being. Jesus shared our weaknesses and problems. By voluntarily accepting the worst kind of human suffering—death by crucifixion—he freed us from the grip of the forces inside and outside us that would lead us into sin and away from God (Romans 5–8).

In Paul's understanding, Jesus suffered *for us* in two senses. In one sense, he suffered *instead of us,* so that we do not have to suffer. He brought us forgiveness, so that we do not have to suffer the separation from God that results from sin (Romans 5:6–11). In another sense, Jesus suffered *for us* by making his suffering a gift to us. He accepted the cross out of love for us; now he invites us to share in his love by sharing in his suffering. We share his suffering by accepting the hardships that come our way as we follow him (see Colossians 1:24). When we go through suffering in union with him, trusting in him and uniting our suffering to his, his love grows in us.

We can see this happening in Paul. He has responded to God's invitation to serve as an apostle. As he pursues his assignment, he has run into many difficulties. These, Paul realizes, are Jesus' sufferings overflowing into his life (1:5).

As he shares in Jesus' sufferings, Paul experiences "consolation" from Jesus (1:6). The Greek words translated "consolation" and "console" here (1:3–7) do not refer to sympathy but to encouragement—giving courage, giving strength. In the Greek text of 1:6, Paul says literally that the consolation is "at work" in him. God gives him courage to handle his difficulties.

The Corinthian Christians experience the same dynamic. Like Paul—in fact, through Paul's preaching—they have become joined to Christ. So they experience "the same sufferings" (1:6), that is, the sufferings of Christ. In the New Revised Standard Version of the Bible (the translation that we are using in this guide), Paul says to the Corinthians, "as you share in our sufferings, so also you share in our consolation" (1:7). The word *our* has been added by the translators. More literally, in the Greek text, Paul says, "as you are sharers in the sufferings, so also in the consolation." He means that as the Corinthians share in Jesus' sufferings, they share in the consolation that God gives those who share the sufferings of his Son.

Paul shows us that, for Christians, suffering is not an individualistic thing. He and the Corinthians are joined with Christ and, in Christ, with one another. So Paul's sufferings for Christ in Ephesus somehow benefit the Christians in Corinth, and the consolation he receives from Christ somehow overflows to them. There is a mysterious sharing of both suffering and encouragement among the members of Christ's body. It is as though we were stockholders in a corporation, sharing all the profits and losses.

1:8–11. Paul speaks about his recent suffering. In verse 9, he says, literally, "we *had received* the sentence of death." Perhaps Paul means that he has contracted a fatal illness. Whatever the cause of his suffering, it was serious, and Paul staggered under the weight of it. "We despaired of life itself" (1:8), he says, meaning that he thought he was going to die. Notice that Paul does not put on a show of strength; he does not present himself as Mr. Tough Guy. Rather, he wants the Corinthians to know not only that he suffered but that he was weak in the face of the suffering. He tells them straight out that his sufferings drove him to the brink of despair. "I couldn't cope with it," Paul says. "It was more than I could handle" (see 1:8). Only if the Corinthians see his weakness can they grasp how he experienced God's help—and learn how they can find God's help in the midst of their own weaknesses and sufferings.

"God allowed me to suffer in order to lead me to rely on him more deeply," Paul tells the Corinthians (see 1:9). By coming face-to-face with death, he learned a lesson about God's help. Paul left self-reliance on one side and despair on the other, and put his trust in God (1:8–9).

Earlier Paul spoke of encouragement from God (1:3–7) but did not say exactly what the encouragement consisted of. In verses 9 and 10 he shows us the content of his encouragement: confidence that Christ, who has risen from the dead, will also raise us up into his eternal life. For Paul, this is the core of Christian consolation. Thus, when he spoke earlier about enduring patiently (see 1:6), he did not mean that the Corinthians should just keep their heads down and wait for the storms to pass. He meant that they should actively put their trust in God, believing that God will act for good in their suffering and by raising them from the dead, will ultimately vanquish evil and sorrow.

Partnership in Christ creates a community of suffering, of encouragement, and of prayer. Paul thanks God on behalf of the Corinthians (1:3–7), and he asks them, in turn, to pray for him (1:10–11).

Reflections. Jesus suffered the full effects of the world's opposition to God's will. He let this opposition crush him; he accepted death on a cross. Yet, by being crushed, he crushed the power of opposition to God—Satan, sin, and death. If we are willing to share in his suffering, our suffering will play a part in his kingdom coming in the world and touching the people around us (see Colossians 1:24–29).

It may be easier to see God's kingdom advancing in the world through Paul's suffering than through ours. Constantly making missionary journeys and enduring persecution, Paul labors and suffers in his apostolic efforts to bring the good news about Jesus to people. Very few of us have Paul's focused sense of Christian mission. Our hardships and pains tend to be more ordinary, less "apostolic" than Paul's. Rather than being arrested and beaten for preaching the gospel, we lose a job or a loved one, or suffer rejection by a spouse or child, or develop a debilitating disease. Can these sufferings be a sharing in Jesus' suffering? They can, because Jesus has united us with himself. Because we are united with him by faith and baptism, we are members of his body. Thus he shares the sufferings we encounter, and our sufferings become ways of sharing in his sufferings—and opportunities to experience his encouragement.

Often, when things go wrong, we do not feel close to the Lord. But notice that Paul does not say that in his recent troubles *he* felt a powerful sense of connection with Jesus. Actually, he says that he felt "utterly, unbearably crushed" (1:8). It does not sound as if he had a sense of close attachment to Jesus then—or, if he did, it does not seem to have given him serenity. For Paul, as for us, suffering is suffering. Sometimes what is most painful for us is the apparent absence of the kind God who previously showered us with blessings. In some cases—the sickness of infants, for example— we may simply be incapable of imagining how God might *ever* use such suffering for good. But again, Paul does not suggest that we can always grasp how our sufferings are a sharing in Christ's or how they will serve the coming of his kingdom.

It may be worth reflecting that, if our union with Jesus' sufferings is unseen and deeply mysterious, that does not make it different in principle from every other aspect of our relationship with him. In the Christian life, we always proceed on the basis of faith. We always face the challenge of trusting God in regard to things we cannot see—or can see only partially and fleetingly (1 Corinthians 13:12). Paul offers his own experience as an example of growing in trust in the "God who raises the dead" (1:9). This trust is a form of hope—and hope is a strange plant. Sown in the daytime, when the sunshine of God's love seems to fill the world with his presence, hope matures and bears fruit in the dark night, when God may seem to have abandoned us in our weakness and pain.

Questions for Application

40 minutes
Choose questions according to your interest and time.

1   Paul twice calls Jesus "Lord" (1:2–3). What does it mean for you personally to call Jesus "Lord"?

2   How have you experienced consolation and encouragement from God? What difference has it made in your life? Where do you feel the need for it now? Where is God challenging you to learn (more deeply) the lesson Paul learned in 1:9?

3   Paul regards his sufferings as a share in the sufferings of Christ, to be endured with patience and hope in the resurrection (1:9). Yet he hopes that God will rescue him from suffering and imminent death (1:10). How do these two attitudes go together?

4   In his own distress, Paul was a channel of God's encouragement to the Corinthians. When have your own difficulties and hardships put you in a position to comfort and help another person? Where might God be calling you to do this today?

5   When has someone's willingness to suffer for Christ and for others been a source of encouragement for you? How could you follow their example?

6 For personal reflection: Paul was willing to talk about his weakness in the face of difficulties. Are you? Are there weaknesses that you would rather not think about or deal with? Is there help, guidance, or support available that you are not taking advantage of? Discuss your reflections with God.

7 Describe an experience when you have been part of a group—a department at work, a military unit, a sports team, whatever—where everybody helped each other in the hard places and there was a lot of encouragement. How could you help to bring this spirit to your family, work environment, or parish?

8 Is it always possible to comfort another person? What else can we do when we are forced to watch another person suffer and cannot alleviate their pain? What has been your experience in giving comfort? in receiving comfort? What "works"? What doesn't?

Approach to Prayer

15 minutes
Use this approach—or create your own!

♦ Paul's statement "on him we have set our hope that he will rescue us again" (1:10) may be an echo of Psalm 22:4–5: "In you our ancestors trusted; . . . in you they trusted, and were not put to shame." Jesus began to pray this psalm on the cross (see Mark 15:34). One way to pray this psalm is as a reminder of Jesus' suffering on our behalf. Since the psalm moves from urgent appeal (Psalm 22:1–21) to celebration of God's faithfulness (Psalm 22:22–31), it also reminds us of Jesus' confidence in God. Take a minute to reflect on Jesus' sufferings, on those of someone you know, and on any difficulties you yourself are experiencing. Then, united with Christ, pray Psalm 22 together on behalf of all who suffer.

Saints in the Making

Better Able to Comfort

This section is a supplement for individual reading.

In her twenties, Jean Haines worked with children as a physical therapist. Her training enabled her to help children with serious disabilities learn to deal with their limitations. Sometimes they asked hard questions. "Why was I born this way?" "Why did God let this happen to me?" It was not easy to comfort a child with a lifetime disability, Jean says. "I could say, 'Yes, I know you must be frustrated.' But the child would think, 'She doesn't really know. She can run around the block.'"

When she was thirty, Jean developed signs of multiple sclerosis. For a while she continued her work as a physical therapist. As MS reduced her mobility, she took a less-strenuous job, testing children for brain damage. After a few years, she retired.

While MS prevented Jean from helping children as she had done before, she found that it opened a door that earlier had been closed. "It's easier to say, 'I know what it's like,' to a disabled person when they know that you have really experienced the kind of pain that they are going through," she says.

Jean's message is more than one of sympathy. She works with an association called Victorious Missionaries, which is run by people with disabilities who want to help others with disabilities recognize their potential. "We want disabled people to understand that they have gifts too and to use them for the greater good," Jean says.

Six times a year, the branch of Victorious Missionaries in which Jean is involved, in Flushing, Michigan, hosts a daylong retreat for people with any sort of physical or mental disability. Through Scripture passages appropriate to the liturgical season, the retreats help participants see the light of Christ, Jean explains, and "encourage and empower them to bring the light of Christ to other people."

The members of the Victorious Missionaries tell the participants how their own disabilities have not prevented them from becoming better people, from praying and helping others. Having MS gives her credibility, Jean says. "Because of my disability, people ask themselves, 'What does she have, that she is happy?' 'Who is this God that she loves so much?' 'There must be something to her message.'"

THE POWER AND THE GLORY

Questions to Begin

15 minutes
Use a question or two to get warmed up for the reading.

1 Do you like processions and parades? What's your favorite— or least favorite?

2 When have you needed a letter of recommendation? Did it give you the help you needed?

5 minutes
Read the passage aloud. Let individuals take turns reading
paragraphs.

What's Happening

It seems that some Christian missionaries who are unfriendly to
Paul have arrived in Corinth and have stirred up suspicions about
his qualifications and motives. In response, Paul affirms that he
has related to the Corinthians in an honest manner (1:12). He tries
to clear up a misunderstanding over why he canceled the promised
visit (1:15–2:2) and assures anyone who may have offended him of
his forgiveness (2:5–11).

Continuing to defend himself, Paul now speaks about his
role as an apostle. He explains why he experiences tremendous
confidence in carrying out his apostolic assignment. His explanation
tells us much about God's power in human weakness.

The Reading: 2 Corinthians 2:14–4:6

A Role in God's Plans

2:14 Thanks be to God, who in Christ always leads us in triumphal
procession, and through us spreads in every place the fragrance
that comes from knowing him. 15 For we are the aroma of Christ to
God among those who are being saved and among those who are
perishing; 16 to the one a fragrance from death to death, to the other
a fragrance from life to life. Who is sufficient for these things? 17 For
we are not peddlers of God's word like so many; but in Christ we
speak as persons of sincerity, as persons sent from God and standing
in his presence.

3:1 Are we beginning to commend ourselves again? Surely we
do not need, as some do, letters of recommendation to you or from
you, do we? 2 You yourselves are our letter, written on our hearts,
to be known and read by all; 3 and you show that you are a letter of
Christ, prepared by us, written not with ink but with the Spirit of the
living God, not on tablets of stone but on tablets of human hearts.

4 Such is the confidence that we have through Christ toward
God. 5 Not that we are competent of ourselves to claim anything
as coming from us; our competence is from God, 6 who has made
us competent to be ministers of a new covenant, not of letter but of
spirit; for the letter kills, but the Spirit gives life.

A Reason for Confidence

7 Now if the ministry of death, chiseled in letters on stone tablets, came in glory so that the people of Israel could not gaze at Moses' face because of the glory of his face, a glory now set aside, 8 how much more will the ministry of the Spirit come in glory? 9 For if there was glory in the ministry of condemnation, much more does the ministry of justification abound in glory! 10 Indeed, what once had glory has lost its glory because of the greater glory; 11 for if what was set aside came through glory, much more has the permanent come in glory!

12 Since, then, we have such a hope, we act with great boldness, 13 not like Moses, who put a veil over his face to keep the people of Israel from gazing at the end of the glory that was being set aside. 14 But their minds were hardened. Indeed, to this very day, when they hear the reading of the old covenant, that same veil is still there, since only in Christ is it set aside. 15 Indeed, to this very day whenever Moses is read, a veil lies over their minds; 16 but when one turns to the Lord, the veil is removed. 17 Now the Lord is the Spirit, and where the Spirit of the Lord is, there is freedom. 18 And all of us, with unveiled faces, seeing the glory of the Lord as though reflected in a mirror, are being transformed into the same image from one degree of glory to another; for this comes from the Lord, the Spirit.

A Light That Gives Courage

4:1 Therefore, since it is by God's mercy that we are engaged in this ministry, we do not lose heart. 2 We have renounced the shameful things that one hides; we refuse to practice cunning or to falsify God's word; but by the open statement of the truth we commend ourselves to the conscience of everyone in the sight of God. 3 And even if our gospel is veiled, it is veiled to those who are perishing. 4 In their case the god of this world has blinded the minds of the unbelievers, to keep them from seeing the light of the gospel of the glory of Christ, who is the image of God. 5 For we do not proclaim ourselves; we proclaim Jesus Christ as Lord and ourselves as your slaves for Jesus' sake. 6 For it is the God who said, "Let light shine out of darkness," who has shone in our hearts to give the light of the knowledge of the glory of God in the face of Jesus Christ.

Questions for Careful Reading

10 minutes
Choose questions according to your interest and time.

1 In 2:17 and 3:1, Paul may be making indirect references to other missionaries and their methods. What does he seem to suggest about their motives and methods?

2 How could Paul's announcement of the good news about Jesus be both "a fragrance from death to death" to some and "a fragrance from life to life" to others (2:16)?

3 Locate Paul's references to "glory." What does he seem to mean by this word?

4 Paul seems to acknowledge that no one is "sufficient" to act as God's representative (see 2:16). Why, then, is he so confident in acting as God's representative (3:4, 12; 4:1)?

5 What transformation is Paul talking about in 3:18? How does it happen? to whom? for what purpose?

A Guide to the Reading

If participants have not read this section already, read it aloud. Otherwise go on to "Questions for Application."

Wth its many twists and turns, this is the kind of writing by St. Paul that makes eyes glaze over when it is read aloud at Mass. Before diving into the details, it is helpful to step back and get the big picture. In simplest terms, the big picture is this: God is making himself known and sharing his life with men and women through his Son, Jesus Christ.

This picture is already familiar to the Corinthians, who have become Christians through Paul's preaching. Why, then, does he place it before them here? Perhaps other missionaries have accused him of being puffed up and overly self confident. In response, Paul reminds the Corinthians of the big picture of God's action through Christ in the world, in order to explain why he is so bold in carrying out his role in God's plans. Simply, Paul is bold because God's action is great.

Wanting to give the Corinthians a sense of the magnificence of what God is doing through Christ, Paul compares it with God's past activity through Moses. Paul may give the impression here of criticizing the Mosaic covenant. But his comparison assumes that the Mosaic covenant was a very good thing; the surpassing goodness of Christ can be appreciated only by a comparison with something very good. In Paul's mind, the Mosaic law was good because God gave it—a fact confirmed by a divine brilliance that radiated from Moses' face when he acted as the go-between for God and the Israelites in the giving of the law (3:7; see Exodus 34:29–35).

Paul was a lifelong Jew. But he came to see that as good as the Mosaic law is, it fails to meet people's deepest needs. The Mosaic law defines right and wrong, which is useful, but it does not, by itself, give people the power to do right and avoid wrong. Without further help, those who try to follow the law are headed for frustration. Inevitably, in some area of life, they will fail. God's verdict on them will be "guilty." Thus Moses' delivery of the law to the Israelites turned out to be a "ministry of death" (3:7). God did not give the law in order to bring death; but, by setting a standard unattainable by sinful men and women, "the very commandment that promised life proved to be death" (Romans 7:10). The "letter"—Paul's compact way of saying "God's commandments without the power to live them out"—"kills" (3:6).

The Mosaic law summons us to love God with all our heart, mind, and strength (see Deuteronomy 6:5)—to center our thoughts and desires on God, to devote ourselves to God's purposes. Our failures to keep the law show how far we are from being lovers of God. Our flawed responses reveal our need for an inner power to enable us to focus our attention on God, freeing us to treat others as persons deserving our concern and care.

Paul is elated because he realizes that God is making this power and freedom available. The glory of God that was reflected for a while on Moses' face now shines permanently from the face of Jesus. By the Spirit living in us, we can look at Jesus; as we do, God's light shines on us and transforms us (4:6). In this way the Spirit brings us "freedom" from our innate selfism (3:17). God plants in us a desire for what is truly good and gives us the ability to commit ourselves to the good of other people (3:18).

Paul's presentation of these thoughts is not easy to follow. In 3:1, he speaks about "letters of recommendation." Perhaps other missionaries arrived in Corinth with letters of recommendation (from the apostles in Jerusalem?) and raised the question, "Where's Paul's letter of recommendation? He does have one, doesn't he?" Paul replies: "Dear Corinthians, my letter of recommendation is you! You became Christians through my preaching. What better evidence of the genuineness of my apostolic assignment could you have than that?" The Corinthians themselves are a kind of letter of recommendation, written by Christ and delivered by Paul ("prepared"—3:3—could also be translated "delivered"). Up to verse 3:3, Paul contrasts a letter of recommendation written with ink on papyrus with a letter of recommendation written by the Spirit on human hearts. But then, as smoothly as a ballroom dancer, Paul pivots and glides off in a new direction. His comparison is recast as a contrast of two covenants (3:6–7), one engraved on stone tablets (the law God gave to Moses), the other written on human hearts (the covenant through Christ).

No sooner has Paul completed this dazzling maneuver than he presents another complicated comparison, this time between his ministry and that of Moses (3:7–18). Exodus suggests that Moses covered his face so that the people would not have to look at the blinding radiance of God reflected there (Exodus 34:29–35). Paul gives this incident an unexpected interpretation. He says that Moses put on a veil so that the Israelites would not see the *fading* of the radiance—a fading that symbolized the passing of the Mosaic covenant, which was eventually going to be "set aside" with the coming of Christ (3:7). Puzzlingly, Paul does not explain why Moses would not want the people to see the fading of the radiance on his face (3:12–13). In Paul's discussion, the veil is something of a moving target. First it is on Moses' face; then it seems to cover the Mosaic law; finally it is on the minds of Jews when they listen to the Mosaic law read in the synagogue. More fancy footwork!

Paul makes life under the Mosaic law sound pretty bleak. But it is important to recognize that Paul makes his comparison of the Mosaic covenant and the covenant in Christ as black and white as possible in order to show the greatness of the covenant through Christ. Paul is not trying to give a balanced evaluation of spiritual life among the people of Israel under the Mosaic covenant in Old Testament times or later centuries. If we were to point out to Paul that the Old Testament offers much evidence that the Spirit was already active in people's lives under the Mosaic covenant, he might answer, "Sure. But even so, the light given through the Mosaic covenant is almost darkness in comparison with the incomparable brilliance of Christ" (see 3:10).

Reflections. Paul points us toward the power that God offers us as the remedy for our most debilitating weakness—our proneness to sin, our lack of love. Through Christ, God places his Spirit within us. With his power, we can overcome our lack of love for God and one another and become the men and women God has created us to be.

Paul also sheds light on our experience of human weakness in our service to God. What sinful human being could be qualified to be an instrument by which the holy God makes himself known to people? Paul is especially aware of his unsuitability for God's service (2:16): "I am . . . unfit to be called an apostle, because I persecuted the church of God" (1 Corinthians 15:9). Paul knows that he is God's agent only because of God's mercy and forgiveness (4:1). "By the grace of God I am what I am" (1 Corinthians 15:10). This foundation makes Paul more confident in being God's servant.

All of us are called to play a part in the process of God's love coming to the people around us. Like Paul, we too, despite our unworthiness, can trust that God is with us in our efforts to serve him. We too are able to represent God to others because he graciously chooses to make us his representatives. Since it is God's work we are involved in, we can be sure that our efforts will have good results. Our confidence is not in our own abilities but in God's working through us (2:14; 4:6).

At the same time, Paul stands as an example of the limits of the power given by God. Paul is divinely empowered to speak the truth, but he cannot guarantee that anyone will accept it. Paul would love to convert everyone to Christ, but factors outside his control affect people and limit their freedom. Above all, there is the devil (4:4). God gives Paul the strength to present the good news of Jesus honestly and sincerely (2:17; 4:2) but not to determine when, how, or whether people will respond. Some do, others don't (2:15–16; 4:3–4). Paul can only speak the message that God wants him to deliver—and leave the results in God's hands.

Just as the Spirit gives Paul the power to play his part, the Spirit also enables him to resist discouragement when his message is not welcomed. Thus Paul is confident not only when he sees the effects of his service in people's lives (3:3) but also when no results can be seen (3:12–15).

Questions for Application

40 minutes
Choose questions according to your interest and time.

1 When, in a relationship with another person, have you felt like a veil was removed from your eyes and you could see the person in a new way? When have you had this kind of experience in your relationship with God?

2 Does our reading suggest anything about whether the process of transformation in Christ is quick and easy? Based on this reading, what does the process of personal transformation involve? How difficult does it seem?

3 Reread 4:1. What are the signals of your losing heart? Where are you susceptible to temptations of discouragement? What does this reading say to you about this? Can you take some inspiration from Paul's words when you get discouraged?

4 Reread 3:18 and 4:6, where Paul writes about seeing the glory of the Lord. Have you experienced anything like this? What helps you see the glory of the unseen God? Do you find help in looking at statues, pictures, or icons? Do you experience the Mass as an opportunity to gaze upon the unseen?

5 Reread Paul's statements about the Holy Spirit (3:3, 5–6, 7–8, 17, 18). How can a person get to know the Holy Spirit better and be more open to the Spirit's presence?

6 Paul speaks of God commanding light to shine in darkness (4:6). When have you had the experience of God shining light in the darkness?

7 Paul speaks of a veil as an obstacle to perception. When might someone in your life—a parent, teacher, pastor, employer, friend—have felt that there was a veil over your face, preventing you from hearing and understanding what they were saying to you? Have you changed?

8 For personal reflection: Where do you most need the power of the Spirit to help you be the person God wants you to be? What kind of honesty and humility do you need to cooperate with the Spirit? How can you express to God your desire to change and your trust in God's help?

Approach to Prayer

15 minutes
Use this approach—or create your own!

♦ Spend a few minutes in silence. Ask the Holy Spirit to bring to mind areas of your life that especially need transformation. Ask the Spirit to help you cooperate with his transforming work. End by praying together this prayer by John Henry Newman.

Dear Jesus,
Help us to spread your fragrance
    everywhere we go.
Flood our souls with your Spirit
    and life.
Penetrate and possess our whole
    being, so utterly,
        that our lives may only be a
        radiance of yours.
Shine through us, and be so in us,
    that every soul we come in
    contact with
    may feel your presence in
    our soul. . . .
Stay with us, and then we shall
    begin to shine
    as you shine;
So to shine as to be a light to
    others.
The light, O Jesus, will be all
    from you,
    none of it will be ours;
It will be You shining on others
    through us.

Saints in the Making

Supporters in Prayer

This section is a supplement for individual reading.

In 1947 Jacqueline de Decker, a Belgian woman, met Mother Teresa in Calcutta, India, and wanted to join her in her work. But Jacqueline's health was poor, and she was forced to return to Belgium for treatment. Her medical condition turned out to be serious and, despite repeated surgery, she was soon largely disabled. Returning to India was out of the question. Deeply disappointed, de Decker considered suicide. But then she received a letter from Mother Teresa with a proposal: "You have been longing to be a missionary. Why not become spiritually bound to our society which you love so dearly? While we work in the slums, you share in the prayers and the work with your suffering and your prayers. The work here is tremendous and needs workers, it is true, but I also need souls like yours to pray and suffer." At the time, Jacqueline was recovering from surgery. She went around the hospital and invited other patients to join her in responding to Mother Teresa's invitation. Later she formed an informal association called "the link"—linking those who prayed with Mother Teresa's sisters.

Author Kathryn Spink visited Jacqueline de Decker and made this report. "By the time I met Jacqueline de Decker, her torso was rigidly encased in a corset and her neck was restricted by a surgical collar. Yet from her home in Antwerp she managed . . . to co-ordinate the link for the sick and suffering. . . . The link . . . brought me into contact with people suffering from every conceivable illness, from elephantiasis to chronic depression. And yet from most, if not all, of these encounters I came away in some unexpected way uplifted. . . . [They] had somehow taken on board Mother Teresa's message that suffering shared with Christ's passion could be a 'wonderful gift,' that the prayers of the suffering had a special potency and that their lives were not therefore devoid of dignity, meaning or purpose. Their letters . . . filled with human frailty as they were, contained nevertheless—or perhaps precisely for that reason—many lessons for me, not least that somehow and sometimes suffering could be the medicine that deepens our humanity. . . . Stripped and weak to the point of being unable even to pray, many were possessed of that most easily lost of all virtues, humility—a genuine belief that they were useless dependants on God alone."

Looking at What Can't Be Seen

Questions to Begin

15 minutes
Use a question or two to get warmed up for the reading.

1 On a scale of one to ten, how "at home" and settled do you feel in your current residence?

2 What are your feelings about spending a vacation camping in a tent?

5 minutes
Read the passage aloud. Let individuals take turns reading
paragraphs.

What's Happening

Paul continues to defend himself as a minister of Christ. Apparently some people in Corinth view his constant hardships as evidence that he is not very spiritual. If he were filled with the power of God's Spirit, they ask, wouldn't he be more successful? Wouldn't fewer disasters befall him? Paul doesn't apologize for his hardships or his apparent powerlessness over circumstances. In his view, his ministry has its credentials not *in spite of* his sufferings but *because* of them. His sufferings are an essential part of being a representative of Jesus, who embraced suffering as the means through which God would act. Paul sees weaknesses and hardships as a natural part of being an apostle, indeed, of being a Christian.

The Reading: 2 Corinthians 4:7–5:10

Experiencing the Power of the Risen Lord

4:7 But we have this treasure in clay jars, so that it may be made clear that this extraordinary power belongs to God and does not come from us. 8 We are afflicted in every way, but not crushed; perplexed, but not driven to despair; 9 persecuted, but not forsaken; struck down, but not destroyed; 10 always carrying in the body the death of Jesus, so that the life of Jesus may also be made visible in our bodies. 11 For while we live, we are always being given up to death for Jesus' sake, so that the life of Jesus may be made visible in our mortal flesh. 12 So death is at work in us, but life in you.

13 But just as we have the same spirit of faith that is in accordance with scripture—"I believed, and so I spoke"—we also believe, and so we speak, 14 because we know that the one who raised the Lord Jesus will raise us also with Jesus, and will bring us with you into his presence. 15 Yes, everything is for your sake, so that grace, as it extends to more and more people, may increase thanksgiving, to the glory of God.

Looking Forward to Resurrection

16 So we do not lose heart. Even though our outer nature is wasting away, our inner nature is being renewed day by day. 17 For this slight momentary affliction is preparing us for an eternal weight of glory beyond all measure, 18 because we look not at what can be seen but at what cannot be seen; for what can be seen is temporary, but what cannot be seen is eternal.

5:1 For we know that if the earthly tent we live in is destroyed, we have a building from God, a house not made with hands, eternal in the heavens. 2 For in this tent we groan, longing to be clothed with our heavenly dwelling—3 if indeed, when we have taken it off we will not be found naked. 4 For while we are still in this tent, we groan under our burden, because we wish not to be unclothed but to be further clothed, so that what is mortal may be swallowed up by life. 5 He who has prepared us for this very thing is God, who has given us the Spirit as a guarantee.

6 So we are always confident; even though we know that while we are at home in the body we are away from the Lord— 7 for we walk by faith, not by sight. 8 Yes, we do have confidence, and we would rather be away from the body and at home with the Lord. 9 So whether we are at home or away, we make it our aim to please him. 10 For all of us must appear before the judgment seat of Christ, so that each may receive recompense for what has been done in the body, whether good or evil.

10 minutes
Choose questions according to your interest and time.

1 Based on what he said in last week's reading, what does Paul mean here by "this treasure" (4:7)?

2 What do you think Paul is trying to communicate by his images of clay pots and tents? What are some similarities between clay pots and tents? If he were writing today, what images from modern life might Paul have used instead?

3 How is Jesus' life "made visible" in Paul (4:10) as he goes through the experiences he describes in 4:8–9?

4 It seems self-contradictory to speak about *looking at* what *cannot be seen* (4:18). How would you explain Paul's meaning here?

5 In 4:8–12, does Paul imply that we should simply welcome suffering and do nothing to escape it or alleviate it? Consider what Paul has said in previous readings.

A Guide to the Reading

If participants have not read this section already, read it aloud. Otherwise go on to "Questions for Application."

4:7–15. At the end of our last reading, Paul triumphantly declared that God "has shone in our hearts to give the light of the knowledge of the glory of God in the face of Jesus Christ" (4:6). But, he continues, this "treasure" is being transported in "clay jars" (4:7). God's "extraordinary power" (4:7) is in weak, mortal men and women. The "clay jars" Paul refers to are ceramic containers used for shipping olive oil and wine. They are cheap and easily broken. Their fragility is uppermost in Paul's mind as he goes on to describe his vulnerabilities (4:8–11).

Bearing the message of Jesus to a largely unreceptive world, Paul encounters opposition and hardships that expose all his human weaknesses. He is "afflicted in every way" (4:8). His sufferings are psychological as well as physical: at times, he is "perplexed"—disturbed, bewildered. Paul uses two forms of the same word when he writes "perplexed" and not "driven to despair"; his words could be translated "at a loss, but not totally at a loss." He is "struck down, but not destroyed" (4:9)—we might say "knocked down, but not knocked out."

Paul is trying to get us to see two sides of a deep paradox. The all-powerful Spirit of the creator lives in us, yet we remain vulnerable—that is, "woundable"—creatures. Paul does not bemoan this paradox because the unrelenting exposure of his weaknesses allows the "extraordinary power" that God has placed in his human clay to become evident. As Paul suffers blow after blow but goes on with his work, it becomes apparent to people that he is held together by an invisible power (4:7).

The paradox of the power of God in Paul's weakness—and in ours—is rooted in Jesus, who was crucified in weakness and rose in power. Jesus now opens his suffering to us, as a kind of place where he makes his power present. Paul vividly expresses this sharing in Jesus' suffering and power by saying that we are "always carrying in the body the death of Jesus, so that the life of Jesus may also be made visible in our bodies" (4:10). Jesus' risen life is made visible in Paul not only in the power that enables him to persevere

but also in the love that overflows from him to those he serves
(4:11–12).

While Paul's sufferings are a sharing in Jesus' sufferings,
they are still *Paul's* sufferings, different from those Jesus
experienced. On the one hand, the Gospels never show Jesus being
at a loss or bewildered, but Paul sometimes is. On the other hand,
Jesus experienced being "forsaken" by God on the cross (Mark
15:34), while Paul never experiences being "forsaken" (4:9). Just as
Paul's particular sufferings were different from those of Jesus, ours
may be different from theirs. We might be more—or less—subject
to despondency than Paul. We may have family sorrows—the birth
of a child with cystic fibrosis, the death of a spouse—that Jesus
never experienced. Each of us suffers in our own way. Nevertheless,
our sufferings become a sharing in Jesus' sufferings, a bearing of
his death (see 4:10), through our union with him by faith.

Paul rates his afflictions as "slight" compared to the
joy of God's kingdom (4:17). Nevertheless, he does not give
the impression of being a person who finds afflictions easy to
bear (4:8–9). A man who sometimes feels "crushed" and driven
almost to despair (1:8) has not found a formula for rising above
his problems. Paul does not float peacefully over troubled waters.
Sometimes, perhaps, the evidence of God's power at work in him is
simply that he doesn't throw in the towel.

A philosopher in Paul's day named Epictetus wrote that
hardships show what a person truly is—they expose the person's
inner character. In Paul's view, difficulties reveal not so much our
inner character as that of God. Our hardships are an opportunity
for God to show his power (4:7, 10). This is not to deny the
importance of human strength of character. From the hardships
that Paul endured, it is obvious that he was a man of determination,
endurance, and courage. But Paul recognizes that such human
qualities are not enough. On a recent occasion, he admitted, he
would have despaired if God had not intervened (1:8–9). He talks
about God's encouragement frequently (1:4–7; 7:6–7, 13) because
he needs it.

4:16–5:10. Paul reflects on our complex nature: we are weak and mortal, yet capable of being filled with God's Spirit and living with God forever. Paul calls our weak aspect the "outer nature" (4:16)—symbolized as a fragile clay jar (see 4:7) or an insecure, temporary "tent" (5:1–4). By "outer nature" Paul means our whole bodily, human makeup, including our mind—the part of us that gets "perplexed" (4:8). Our "inner nature" (4:16) is also our whole person, seen in terms of our capacity for a relationship with God. It is our heart, will, and character—the aspect of us by which we make moral decisions (see Romans 7:22; Ephesians 3:16). Our inner person can—and does—go wrong, recognizing the rightness of God's will but turning away from it (Romans 7:22–24).

Our outer and inner natures are not separate parts of us but different dimensions—like the length and width of a picture. Our fragile outer dimension is an essential aspect of our humanity, an aspect of our likeness to God (see Genesis 1:26). The jar, or tent, of our outer nature is an essential aspect of our true self, not a mere container or covering. Yet, sadly, it is wearing out, in the course of our service to Christ (as in Paul's experience in 4:8–9) and simply with the passage of time.

Yet, Paul encourages us. We have cause for joy because of what is happening inside us. Our inner nature is being renewed by the presence of Christ and the Spirit (4:16; Ephesians 3:16; 4:24; Colossians 3:10). Already, God is making us new (5:17; Galatians 6:15) and preparing us for eternal life (4:17) by empowering a process of growth. "Seeing the glory of the Lord as though reflected in a mirror, [we] are being transformed into the same image from one degree of glory to another; for this comes from the Lord, the Spirit" (3:18).

As complex, inner/outer creatures, our ultimate goal is not to jettison our outer nature and liberate ourselves from the body with its sufferings. Our outer dimension, after it wears out in death, is to be renewed and restored in the final resurrection. Paul looks forward to his mortal dimension being "swallowed up by life" (5:4). After folding our earthly tent in death, we are to wake up with our tent set up anew in the courtyard of the great heavenly temple, where it will be secure forever, beyond the reach of any storms that could cause it to wear out or collapse (5:1–2). To give us confidence in this future life, God has given us his Spirit as a "guarantee," or down payment (5:5).

Paul got into this discussion of afflictions and power, of our outer and inner natures, in an attempt to explain why he is bold in his apostolic work. In the face of opposition and hardships, experiencing vulnerabilities and weaknesses, he sees his earthly life getting worn down, even feels crushed and forsaken. Yet he does not "lose heart" (4:16). He is "always confident" (5:6; see also 5:8) because he experiences the Spirit changing him, readying him for God's kingdom, leading him to desire it and hope for it.

The certainty that God will bring a new creation, where men and women will enjoy harmony and fulfillment, gives Paul the ability to keep going through suffering (4:16–18). He lives by this inner vision of Christ and his kingdom, generated by the Spirit in him (4:6; 5:7). No matter how troubles weigh him down, he is buoyed by the confidence that he is going home to the Lord (5:8).

Reflections. Paul has spoken about having faith in God who raises the dead (1:9). Now he has shown us that this means both depending on God to help us here and now—such as rescuing us from dangers (1:10)—*and* fixing our attention on our ultimate goal, resurrection and life in God's kingdom (4:16–18). We cannot know what God will and will not do in our lives or in this world. Indeed, we may sometimes be "perplexed" by our experience and by what we see around us. But no matter what happens, we can be sure that God's kingdom is coming toward us and that God invites us to share in it. This is the fundamental reason not to lose heart.

Questions for Application

40 minutes
Choose questions according to your interest and time.

1 When has difficulty or suffering led you to a deeper trust in God? How could you put that trust to work in an area of your life today?

2 Have you ever experienced anything like what Paul describes in 4:8–9? How did this experience affect you?

3 When have you seen evidence that God was helping a person get through their difficulties? What can you learn from their faith?

4 Paul views his difficulties both as an opportunity for God to reveal his love to people here and now (4:7–11) and as a preparation for eternal life (4:16–18). When you have difficulties, do you take either of these approaches? How could you apply one of Paul's approaches to a situation in your life?

5 Among people you have known, who stands as an example of taking Paul's approach to difficulties? What could you learn from them?

6 How can Christians help each other grow in dealing with weakness and suffering?

7 For personal reflection: Do you ever think about dying? What do you believe will happen to you when you die? Do you have confidence—as Paul does—in resurrection in Christ? How does your confidence—or lack of it—affect how you live? What could you do to deepen your faith in Christ and in his love?

Approach to Prayer

15 minutes
Use this approach—or create your own!

♦ Take time to intercede for the needs of participants and other people, of your parish, and of the Church. Let participants mention brief petitions aloud. After each petition, the group may pray the refrain: "Lord, we do not lose heart. We place our confidence in you." End with an Our Father and a Glory to the Father.

Saints in the Making

Difficulties Are Mere Playthings

This section is a supplement for individual reading.

Frances Xavier Cabrini (1850–1917) was the first citizen of the United States to be declared a saint by the Catholic Church. In 1880, in her native Italy, she founded a religious congregation called the Missionary Sisters of the Sacred Heart of Jesus. Then, in 1889, she took a handful of the sisters with her to New York. Over the next twenty-eight years, she opened orphanages and schools in New York, New Orleans, Denver, and Los Angeles and hospitals in New York, Chicago, and Seattle—where she became a U.S. citizen in 1909. Though she suffered poor health throughout her life and stood a mere five feet tall, frail Mother Cabrini had a will of steel and a relentless dedication to serving the spiritual and material needs of immigrants, particularly Italian immigrants, especially children, the destitute, and the sick. She was bold in initiating big projects and asking people for help, combining business shrewdness with deep faith in God's generosity. Mother Cabrini traveled constantly and wrote many letters to her sisters. Here is a brief excerpt, in the spirit of 2 Corinthians, written in 1896 while she was aboard a ship caught in a storm between Panama and Chile.

The winds roar, heaven darkens, the waves arise and threaten to turn the steamer topsy-turvy. All this matters nothing. I have given my trust, I must keep my word of honor, and with faith and confidence. Difficulties! What are they, Daughters? They are the mere playthings of children enlarged by our imagination, not yet accustomed to focus itself on the Omnipotent. Dangers, dangers! And what are dangers? The spectres that surprise the soul, which having given itself to God, or thinking it has done so, still retains the spirit of the world. . . . "But I am weak!" Who is not weak? But with God's help you can do everything. He never fails the humble and faithful. "Yes, but I am so fragile!" We are all fragile, yet, when Christ is our strength, what shall we fear? "I have failed in generosity, I have fallen at the first temptation, now I shall not be able to do anything well." Have you fallen? Then, humble yourself, and with a live act of contrition from the depths of your heart, ask pardon, renew your promises to God, then get on your feet and be doing with more courage than ever to repair your defects!

HUMILITY: A KIND OF WEAKNESS?

Questions to Begin

15 minutes
Use a question or two to get warmed up for the reading.

1 Can you remember a situation in which you were surprised to discover that someone had misunderstood something you had said or misinterpreted something you had done?

2 Can you remember a situation in which you discovered you had misunderstood what someone else had said or done?

5 minutes
Read the passage aloud. Let individuals take turns reading
paragraphs.

What's Happened

After our reading in Week 3, Paul goes on to explain that he brings
a simple message to men and women everywhere: God has opened
the door to reconciliation with himself through Jesus' death and
resurrection. So be reconciled with God! (see 5:11–6:2). Then
Paul devotes attention to a relief effort he has launched to help
Christians in Jerusalem, where there is a famine. This section
(chapters 8–9) shows how the Church can act as a community of
suffering and encouragement in Christ.

  Now, in chapter 10, Paul's letter takes an unexpected turn.
Up to this point, Paul has used patient explanations to resolve the
problems between himself and the Corinthians. He has seemed
hopeful that the misunderstandings will soon be cleared away
(2:3–10; 7:2–16). In our reading this week, however, the relationship
between Paul and the Corinthians seems to be in a deeper crisis
than ever. Apparently criticism of Paul by other missionaries is
undermining the Corinthians' confidence in him. Perhaps thinking
that the situation has deteriorated so much that it may not be
possible to set things right, Paul makes what one scholar calls a
"desperate counterattack," with dramatic appeals, threats, and
sarcasm.

The Reading: 2 Corinthians 10

Too Meek and Mild to Be an Apostle?

10:1 I myself, Paul, appeal to you by the meekness and gentleness
of Christ—I who am humble when face to face with you, but bold
toward you when I am away!— 2 I ask that when I am present I
need not show boldness by daring to oppose those who think we are
acting according to human standards. 3 Indeed, we live as human
beings, but we do not wage war according to human standards;
4 for the weapons of our warfare are not merely human, but they
have divine power to destroy strongholds. We destroy arguments

5 and every proud obstacle raised up against the knowledge of God, and we take every thought captive to obey Christ. 6 We are ready to punish every disobedience when your obedience is complete.

7 Look at what is before your eyes. If you are confident that you belong to Christ, remind yourself of this, that just as you belong to Christ, so also do we. 8 Now, even if I boast a little too much of our authority, which the Lord gave for building you up and not for tearing you down, I will not be ashamed of it. 9 I do not want to seem as though I am trying to frighten you with my letters. 10 For they say, "His letters are weighty and strong, but his bodily presence is weak, and his speech contemptible." 11 Let such people understand that what we say by letter when absent, we will also do when present.

Are Other Missionaries Better Than Paul?

12 We do not dare to classify or compare ourselves with some of those who commend themselves. But when they measure themselves by one another, and compare themselves with one another, they do not show good sense. 13 We, however, will not boast beyond limits, but will keep within the field that God has assigned to us, to reach out even as far as you. 14 For we were not overstepping our limits when we reached you; we were the first to come all the way to you with the good news of Christ. 15 We do not boast beyond limits, that is, in the labors of others; but our hope is that, as your faith increases, our sphere of action among you may be greatly enlarged, 16 so that we may proclaim the good news in lands beyond you, without boasting of work already done in someone else's sphere of action. 17 "Let the one who boasts, boast in the Lord." 18 For it is not those who commend themselves that are approved, but those whom the Lord commends.

10 minutes
Choose questions according to your interest and time.

1 Paul refers to "such people" (10:11) and to "some" (10:12) who are saying things he doesn't agree with. From this reading, what might these people be saying about themselves? about Paul? How might their attitudes and values be different from Paul's?

2 Nowadays, some readers view Paul as grouchy and overbearing. Yet here he identifies himself with "the meekness and gentleness of Christ" (10:1). What impression of Paul's personality do you get from this reading and from our earlier readings? Be specific about what gives you this impression.

3 Paul speaks about using his pastoral authority to correct problems in the church in Corinth (10:1–11). Does he seem eager to use his authority?

A Guide to the Reading

If participants have not read this section already, read it aloud. Otherwise go on to "Questions for Application."

10:1–6. Apparently some outsiders have been criticizing Paul to his Corinthian converts. In Paul's words here, we may be able to hear what the critics have been saying. The statement in 10:1—"I who am humble when face to face with you, but bold toward you when I am away!"—probably reflects their criticism: "Paul is passive-aggressive. He's very mild and agreeable when he's here in person but acts tough and judgmental when he's at a distance." Verse 10— "His letters are weighty and strong, but his bodily presence is weak, and his speech contemptible"—seems to be a direct quotation of the critics' words.

Paul has been relating to the Corinthians with "meekness and gentleness"—the Greek words mean that he has not projected a sense of self-importance and has made allowances for people's failings. He has shown a tolerant attitude toward those who cause problems, rather than getting impatient with them and losing his temper. He has been "humble" toward the Corinthians (10:1)— seeking to serve them rather than control them.

This way of relating to people may strike us as admirable, and so it may surprise us that it would expose Paul to criticism. But humility was not appreciated in the ancient Mediterranean world. A humble person came across as cringing and groveling; he or she seemed to lack a proper sense of self-worth. People— especially men—were expected to gain honor for themselves and their families, not to be indifferent to it. Paul's humility seemed undignified to the Corinthians.

Some people are apparently claiming that Paul conducts himself "according to human standards"—more literally, in the Greek, "according to the flesh." The allegation here, it seems, is that Paul acts in a weak and cowardly way. When he is far away, he makes heavy demands in his letters; when he is present, he seems timid and unassertive (10:1). This is interpreted by some people (intruding missionaries?) as proof that he lacks the power of the Holy Spirit—that he is "fleshy" rather than spiritual. According to the expectations of the culture, the Corinthians assume that a truly spiritual person would act in a demanding and authoritarian way and would show off his spiritual superiority.

Paul, it seems, is reluctant to exercise his pastoral authority. He prefers to deal with people in a mild manner, using explanation and encouragement rather than issuing commands or meting out punishments. To some people in Corinth, this approach is taken as evidence that he doesn't have any authority and lacks the spiritual qualifications for Christian leadership.

In Paul's own mind, humility is a sign of true spirituality because it is in imitation of Christ. To others, however, it looks like evidence that Paul lacks spiritual authority and power. Paul will address this conflict of values in our readings over the next two weeks. His immediate concern here, however, is to assert that, no matter what anyone says about him, he *does* have pastoral authority. If pressed, he is willing to use it (10:2–6).

Paul's sabre-rattling rhetoric sounds fierce. But the weapons he is speaking about are not swords, but words—the words of Christian preaching and teaching. Even if he switches from persuasion to rebuke, he is not planning to do anyone physical harm. It is ideas, not persons, that he will take captive (10:5). If and when the Corinthians reaffirm their loyalty to Christ ("when your obedience is complete"), he will deal with the intruders who have mocked him as cowardly and weak ("we are ready to punish every disobedience"—10:6).

10:7–11. Paul returns to a point he made earlier when he responded to the Corinthians' question as to whether he had a letter of introduction from higher church authorities (3:1–3). If you want evidence that I am really sent by Christ, Paul says, "look at what is before your eyes" (10:7). Look at yourselves. You're Christians, aren't you? Well, how did that happen? Wasn't it through my preaching of the gospel? Isn't that sufficient evidence that I have been authorized by Christ?

10:12–18. Paul's talk about measures, limits, and spheres of action seems jumbled. His logic is obscure. What does boasting have to do with keeping within assigned limits?

The confusion probably arises from Paul's conducting an indirect argument with the intruding missionaries.

Paul argues that Corinth is his "sphere of action" (10:15), assigned to him by God. The evidence for this claim is that Paul was the first Christian missionary to arrive in Corinth (10:14) and, through his preaching, people believed in Christ and a Christian community came into existence. Thus, whatever his weaknesses and shortcomings, Paul has accomplished something by staying within the "limits" of the sphere of responsibility that God "assigned" to him (10:13–18).

By contrast, the intruders in Corinth have overstepped the limits of their assignment. Paul would probably welcome them in Corinth if they came to help out. He did, in fact, welcome a Christian teacher named Apollos (1 Corinthians 3:6). But these other missionaries are *not* welcome to come into the Christian community and cause dissension. Whatever their assignment might be, it does not involve causing conflict in a Christian community that already has pastoral leadership.

From our reading here, it seems that the intruders are boasting of their forceful personalities and their polished speaking style (see 10:1, 10). In fact, Paul asserts, they have nothing to boast about, because they have gone where they were not sent and have torn down rather than built up. Paul *does* have something to boast about, if he wishes: he went where God sent him, and God worked through him in others' lives (10:15). The standard by which Paul measures himself does not come from himself but from God. The question he asks is not "How well have I fulfilled my own dreams and ambitions?" but "How well have I carried out the responsibilities God assigned to me?" Instead of measuring themselves against each other—competing with each other by their own standards—the other missionaries should measure themselves against the standard of Christ's example (10:12). He is the standard for all his followers.

Reflections. While Paul possesses pastoral authority, he prefers meekness, patience, persuasion, and heartfelt appeals.

He derives satisfaction not from having power over people but from serving them. Nonetheless, he is willing to use his authority if necessary.

Paul is trying to follow the approach to leadership that Jesus taught—an approach that, without eliminating authority, emphasizes humble service (Mark 10:35–45). Jesus didn't say it would be easy to put this approach into practice; Paul could testify, "It's not!" Jesus' approach requires patience and love, which do not come easily to weak human beings. Humility requires the power of the Spirit, especially when opponents criticize it as character weakness, and even as lack of spirituality, as we see happening here.

From this reading, what answer might we give to the question, Is humility a kind of weakness? Clearly, the answer is yes. Humility involves a kind of self-imposed weakness, by which one refrains from advancing one's own interests in order to care for others. And humility certainly *looks* weak, for humble people do not aggressively seek advantages and benefits for themselves. In another sense, however, the answer is no. Humility is not weakness, because it takes strength of will to subordinate one's own needs to the needs of others and to accept the role of servant, especially when doing so brings criticism and scorn.

Questions for Application

40 minutes
Choose questions according to your interest and time.

1 When have you observed someone acting in a way that you consider meek, gentle, or humble? How would you describe the qualities of meekness, gentleness, and humility? How do you see these qualities in Jesus' relationships with people? How have people you've known acted in a meek, gentle, and humble way?

2 Can someone be humble and also be assertive? Do timidity and passivity sometimes look like humility? How can you tell the difference?

3 Select a situation in your life and ask this question: "If I were to be more meek, gentle, or humble, what specifically would I do differently?"

4 Paul has authority, yet in this reading he seems reluctant to exercise it. Have you experienced a similar dilemma? What principles should guide a person in exercising authority?

5 Reflect on the situations in your life where you have authority. Are you exercising it properly? Are there situations where it is best not to try to get something to happen by exercising authority? Are there situations in which it is a mistake *not* to use one's authority?

6 Are you ever tempted to interfere in someone else's sphere of responsibility? How well do you handle the temptation?

7 For personal reflection: Are you ever annoyed when someone else is praised more highly than you think they deserve? when you are praised less than you think you deserve? Do you ever try to compensate for your weaknesses by boasting? Do you ever mentally compare yourself to others? Do you notice other people's weaknesses and compare them to your strengths? Ask God to shed light on this.

Approach to Prayer

15 minutes
Use this approach—or create your own!

♦ Take a few minutes in silence to reflect on question 7 in Questions for Application. Then have someone read the following prayer of St. Thérèse of Lisieux. End with a Glory to the Father.

Lord, you know my weakness. Each morning I resolve to practice humility, and in the evening I recognize that I have committed many faults of pride. Seeing this, I am tempted to get discouraged. Yet I know that discouragement, too, comes from pride. What I therefore want, O my God, is to build my hope on you alone. Since you can do all things, please let the virtue I desire come to birth in my soul. In order to obtain this grace from your infinite mercy, I will often tell you: "Jesus, meek and humble of heart, make my heart like yours."

Saints in the Making

Taking St. Thérèse's Little Way

This section is a supplement for individual reading.

At age nineteen, New York college student Mary Rose Pilsner was diagnosed with cancer. But she was determined to achieve her ambition to become a nurse, and she persevered with her studies at Georgetown University through several surgeries. In 1996, she completed the nursing program with top honors and then achieved a perfect score on the nursing board exam. Three years later, however, signs of the cancer returned, and her condition quickly deteriorated. She died at home in June 1999, at the age of twenty-five.

One of her brothers, Father Peter Pilsner, spoke at her funeral about her short but intense life. She liked basketball and softball, cheerleading, and St. Thérèse of Lisieux. The French saint's autobiography was Mary Rose's favorite book. "My sister did not consider herself 'another Thérèse.' She thought of herself as a disciple of St. Thérèse or as a member of 'her army of little souls,'" Father Pilsner said. "Mary drew strength and inspiration from the life of St. Thérèse and constantly put into practice Thérèse's 'Little Way'"—that is, Thérèse's approach to growing in holiness by taking the small steps of love that each day makes possible, with a deep trust in God's grace.

For Mary Rose, the struggle with cancer and acceptance of death was a little way that required great grace and trust in God.

Father Pilsner drew on some words of St. Paul to express the impression that his sister left on him and his family. "When we encounter someone like Mary, someone who is afflicted, but not crushed; perplexed, but not driven to despair; who is struck down, but not destroyed; who suffers, but does not lose faith . . . we encounter, in a way such as we can neither escape nor deny, the treasure within—the treasure of God's grace in our souls, the treasure of the indwelling Holy Spirit, the treasure of the supernatural life. . . . That is her gift to us."

The Weakness of Being Misunderstood

Questions to Begin

15 minutes
Use a question or two to get warmed up for the reading.

1 What has been your most satisfying experience of working as an unpaid volunteer in the Church or other organization? What made it good?

2 When have you discovered that you underestimated how much someone knew about something? How did you discover your mistake?

What's Happening

Paul continues to defend himself against the criticisms. (If we get tired of reading his self-defenses, imagine how tired of writing them he must have been.) One area of misunderstanding concerns his way of earning a living and his financial relationship—or rather his *lack* of a financial relationship—with the Corinthians. During his time in Corinth, Paul continued his practice of supporting himself by working as a tent maker (Acts 18:1–3; 20:33–35; 1 Corinthians 4:12; 1 Thessalonians 2:5–12; 2 Thessalonians 3:7–9). He refused offers of financial support from the more affluent Corinthian Christians. Probably, he did not want any of them to consider themselves as his special patrons or to think they had a special claim on him. Sometimes the more affluent Corinthians treated the poorer members unfairly (see 1 Corinthians 11:17–22) and got into competition with each other (see 1 Corinthians 3:1–4). In this situation, Paul may have felt that he needed to keep a certain distance from the members who had some financial means, in order to avoid an appearance of favoritism and to maintain his independence as pastor of the whole community. But his policy of self-support as a craftsman and rejection of financial help has not gone over well with everyone, as we see in our reading.

The Reading: 2 Corinthians 11:1–21

Fatherly Concern

11:1 I wish you would bear with me in a little foolishness. Do bear with me! 2 I feel a divine jealousy for you, for I promised you in marriage to one husband, to present you as a chaste virgin to Christ. 3 But I am afraid that as the serpent deceived Eve by its cunning, your thoughts will be led astray from a sincere and pure devotion to Christ. 4 For if someone comes and proclaims another Jesus than the one we proclaimed, or if you receive a different spirit from the one you received, or a different gospel from the one you accepted, you submit to it readily enough.

"He's Not a Very Good Speaker"

5 I think that I am not in the least inferior to these super-apostles. 6 I may be untrained in speech, but not in knowledge; certainly in every way and in all things we have made this evident to you.

"And He Won't Take Money from Us"

7 Did I commit a sin by humbling myself so that you might be exalted, because I proclaimed God's good news to you free of charge? 8 I robbed other churches by accepting support from them in order to serve you. 9 And when I was with you and was in need, I did not burden anyone, for my needs were supplied by the friends who came from Macedonia. So I refrained and will continue to refrain from burdening you in any way. 10 As the truth of Christ is in me, this boast of mine will not be silenced in the regions of Achaia. 11 And why? Because I do not love you? God knows I do!

12 And what I do I will also continue to do, in order to deny an opportunity to those who want an opportunity to be recognized as our equals in what they boast about. 13 For such boasters are false apostles, deceitful workers, disguising themselves as apostles of Christ. 14 And no wonder! Even Satan disguises himself as an angel of light. 15 So it is not strange if his ministers also disguise themselves as ministers of righteousness. Their end will match their deeds.

Angry Sarcasm

16 I repeat, let no one think that I am a fool; but if you do, then accept me as a fool, so that I too may boast a little. 17 What I am saying in regard to this boastful confidence, I am saying not with the Lord's authority, but as a fool; 18 since many boast according to human standards, I will also boast. 19 For you gladly put up with fools, being wise yourselves! 20 For you put up with it when someone makes slaves of you, or preys upon you, or takes advantage of you, or puts on airs, or gives you a slap in the face. 21 To my shame, I must say, we were too weak for that!

10 minutes
Choose questions according to your interest and time.

1 Reread verses 3, 4, 19, and 20. On a scale of 1 to 10 (from bad to good), how would you rate the quality of the relationship between Paul and the Corinthians?

2 In verse 4, Paul speaks of "another Jesus" being preached to the Corinthians. Does he mean that there *is* another Jesus? If not, what is he saying?

3 In verse 19, does Paul really consider the Corinthians "wise"?

4 How might the Corinthians have felt when they read this part of Paul's letter?

A Guide to the Reading

If participants have not read this section already, read it aloud. Otherwise go on to "Questions for Application."

11:1–4. Paul asks the Corinthians to let him get away with a little foolishness (11:1). What foolishness is he planning? He means the foolishness of comparing himself with the missionaries who have intruded themselves into the church in Corinth. They have been comparing him unfavorably to themselves, tearing him down in the Corinthians' eyes (see 10:10). Boasting that his attainments are greater than theirs would be stooping to their level. Paul finds the whole approach of comparing oneself to others a problem because, by putting the focus on human beings, it takes the focus off God. Nevertheless, foolish though it may be, Paul begins to compare himself to these other missionaries: he states that he knows as much as they do (11:5–6) and points out that he has been less of a financial burden on the Corinthians (11:9–15). Paul's boasting here, however, is nothing compared to what he is going to unleash in next week's reading.

Bragging, however, is not Paul's main way of trying to regain the Corinthians' confidence. Mostly he tries to reassure them of his love for them. This is the point of likening himself to a father who has pledged to give his daughter in marriage. New Testament scholar Victor Paul Furnish explains that the imagery here conforms to first-century Jewish marriage customs, "according to which the father of the bride-to-be is responsible for safeguarding his daughter's virginity between the time of her betrothal and the time when he actually leads her into the bridegroom's house." Paul has loved the Corinthians as a father—so they should trust him!

Paul implies that the intruding missionaries have brought "a different gospel" to the Corinthians (11:4)—a different version of the good news about Jesus than the one Paul brought. Yet he does not refute any theological *statements* made by the intruders, so the problem perhaps is not in their *verbal* message about Jesus. In 11:20, Paul remarks that the Corinthians don't object if "someone" tries to dominate or exploit them—probably meaning the intruding missionaries. From Paul's description, it sounds like the intruders are taking advantage of their leadership role to benefit themselves. Thus, their *behavior* reflects a distorted picture of Jesus. They are *living* a "different gospel," even if they are preaching the correct one. If the Corinthians admire and imitate the intruders, they will be "led astray from a sincere and pure devotion to Christ" (11:3), because they will, in effect, be rejecting Jesus, who came not to be served but to serve (Mark 10:45).

11:5–6. One characteristic that makes Paul seem weak in comparison with the "super-apostles" is his unpolished speaking style (11:6). Public speaking was a highly developed form of communication, even entertainment, in the ancient world; greatly admired, a refined speaking style was a matter for pride. Paul admits that he is relatively "untrained" in public speaking (11:6). Remember his earlier reference to what people are saying about him: "his speech [is] contemptible" (10:10). Compared to the super-apostles, he is an amateur at the rostrum. "Hey, keep a sense of proportion," Paul responds. "I may be a poor speaker, but my preaching was good enough for you to come to know Jesus through it." The Corinthians should brush off the intruders' attempt to belittle him, Paul argues. "The fact that I'm an authentic apostle should be obvious to *you*" (see 11:6).

11:7–11. Money is another area where Paul seems weak to the Corinthians. When he lived in Corinth, he declined to accept financial support from them (11:9). We might wonder why this would make them unhappy with him. Wouldn't they be glad that he was not a financial burden? Didn't his approach eliminate suspicions that he was out for material gain? Alas, no. In the Corinthians' eyes, Paul is demeaning himself by his manual work and self-imposed poverty (apparently he sometimes runs out of money—see 11:9). Corinthian Christians who have some money and social standing are embarrassed by their apostle's unseemly behavior. Is this hard to understand? Consider the following: would everyone in your parish be pleased if your pastor refused his salary and took a job driving a tow truck for a local garage? On a more personal level, the Corinthians are offended by Paul's refusal of their offers of financial help—rejecting their money seems to be a rejection of their friendship.

Paul feels strongly that his way of relating to the Corinthians humbly, with an attitude of service, is an accurate reflection of his master, Jesus, who became poor though he was rich so that others might become rich (8:9). But the Corinthians see his behavior as undignified, as a relinquishment of the benefits a wise teacher should enjoy, and even as a lack of love.

11:12–15. Paul rejects the intruding missionaries in strong terms: they are "false apostles, deceitful workers," even ministers of Satan (11:13–14). Despite appearances, Paul does not actually criticize them for accepting financial support for their missionary work. Paul himself wrote that "those who proclaim the gospel should get their living by the gospel" (1 Corinthians 9:14). The problem with these missionaries is that they are going outside their assignment mission field and are making problems in his mission field. They are interfering in the church he has founded (10:12–18) and trying to drive a wedge between him and his converts by bad-mouthing him (10:10). As far as Paul is concerned, they are entitled to draw financial support from those to whom they bring the gospel—but they did not bring the gospel to Corinth and therefore have no right to demand payment from the Christians there.

Since he seems to accept the fact that the intruding missionaries are "ministers of Christ" (11:23), Paul probably thinks that they are tools of Satan *unwittingly.* But because they are seeking to advance their own interests, not the peace and unity of the Church, there is something false about their ministry. They have become instruments of evil, regardless of how talented and credentialed they are or how fine their sermons may be.

If the intruders throw their weight around and use their position for financial gain, as Paul implies (11:20), why do the Corinthians accept them? Apparently the Corinthians expect such behavior from religious teachers. Ambitious, self-seeking behavior is normal in the culture of the time. The Corinthians' acceptance of the intruders gets a sarcastic response from Paul: "You're so wise, you know all about choosing good leaders!" (see 11:19). The sarcasm continues in verse 21: "Well, *excuse me* for being too weak to take advantage of you. Shall I apologize for not ordering you around and making you wait on me?" (see also 11:7). Behind Paul's anger, we can feel the pain of rejection.

Reflections. Instead of gaining him love and trust, Paul's self-sacrificing approach to serving the Corinthians is misinterpreted as lack of love (even as a cover for dishonesty—12:16) and brings him criticism, even scorn. His strong points are dismissed; his shortcomings are mocked (10:10; 11:5–6). We see Paul suffering the weakness of being unable to convince the Corinthians of his good intentions toward them.

Paul has spoken of Satan deceiving unbelievers, blocking their reception of the gospel (2:14–16; 4:1–4). Here we see that believers, too, can be deceived by Satan, who is trying to disrupt Paul's relationship with the Corinthians through deception (11:3, 13–15). Paul experiences weakness in the face of this attack. He can present the Corinthians with the truth about Jesus, and about his own love for them, and appeal to them to believe him. But their response is out of his control.

Earlier Paul told the Corinthians that sometimes he feels "perplexed" (4:8). Did he recall those words as he wrote this part of his letter? He does seem to be at a loss here. The Corinthians should be more convinced than anyone that he is an authentic apostle, yet they are won over by others' arguments that he is a poor apostle, perhaps even a poor Christian. It seems that the only way to convince them that he is no less qualified than the intruders is to put his strengths and accomplishments on display. But such boasting makes no sense for one whose message focuses on Jesus rather than self. What is Paul to do?

In this reading, we see Paul's weaknesses on display. He suffers the weakness of being misunderstood by those he is trying to serve, the weakness of watching those he loves take a wrong path (some parents of adult children will especially sympathize with this aspect of Paul's experience). And we see, again, Paul's determination to imitate the way of his master, Jesus, even if others scorn him as weak for doing so. Paul appreciates the immense importance of reflecting Jesus in his relationships with other people. He knows that, as followers of Jesus, Christians inevitably preach about Jesus by the way they live. Either we offer people a true reflection of our master—or we bring "a different gospel."

Questions for Application

40 minutes
Choose questions according to your interest and time.

1 In this reading we see Paul responding to criticism. He faces difficult situations familiar to all of us: misunderstood motives, unfair criticism, limits to one's ability to gain others' trust. When have you faced these sorts of problems? What wisdom have you gained from these experiences? What can you learn from the way Paul faces these difficulties?

2 Paul is sure that the criticisms leveled at him are misguided and unfair. But sometimes criticism has a grain (or more) of truth in it. How can a person filter out criticism that is inaccurate and unfair while taking seriously criticism that is right on?

3 What kind of return do you expect for your services and kindnesses to others: money? recognition? expressions of gratitude? God's approval? other?

4 Is sarcasm helpful in dealing with misunderstandings between people?

5 From this and earlier readings, what criteria does Paul offer for evaluating the authenticity of those who offer spiritual guidance as teachers, pastors, conference speakers, authors, and media figures?

6 When have you voluntarily declined to use a right or privilege in order to better serve someone? What was the result? What did you learn from the experience?

7 For personal reflection: Paul tries to shape his life in imitation of Jesus. Read Jesus' words about being a servant (Mark 10:35–45) or Paul's words about Jesus (Philippians 2:1–11), and ask yourself how well you are reflecting Jesus to those you live and work with. In what ways are you preaching the real gospel or "a different gospel" to people around you? What steps could you take to imitate Jesus more closely?

Approach to Prayer

15 minutes
Use this approach—or create your own!

♦ Invite the Holy Spirit to guide your thoughts and open your hearts to Jesus' words. Have someone read the Beatitudes aloud (Matthew 5:3–11). After a few moments of silent reflection, pray an Our Father together.

Saints in the Making

Holiness in Rags

This section is a supplement for individual reading.

Despite Paul's weaknesses, he seems in many ways to have been a strong person, with a sharp mind, great determination, and skill in relating to people. Other saints have suffered weaknesses in areas where Paul was strong. A notable example is Benedict Joseph Labré. If Paul was a very together saint, Benedict was a very untogether one.

Born in France in 1748, young Benedict felt drawn to the monastic life. But the various monastic communities on whose doors he knocked refused to take him in or, after welcoming him for a few weeks or months, asked him to leave. He was a restless sort of person who found it impossible to find contentment in a monastic community. From a modern viewpoint, he seems to have been psychologically disturbed. Father Benedict Joseph Groeschel, a noted writer on spiritual life who is also a psychologist—and an admirer of Benedict—has written that Benedict "showed a substantial tendency toward psychosis."

After failing at monastic life, Benedict found his path to God by default. He wandered from shrine to shrine in Europe, living in what one modern writer calls "accidental poverty." Finally he ended up—*settled* would not be quite the right word—in Rome. There he lived as a homeless person, sleeping in the ruins of the Colosseum and visiting churches during the daytime.

In this miserable existence, Benedict found the light of Christ and radiated it to others. He spent time each day praying before the Blessed Sacrament. Father Groeschel writes that Benedict "found the anchor he needed to survive in the Eucharistic presence. . . . He needed several hours of prayer in the presence of Christ every day to cope with life." To fellow homeless people, Benedict showed generosity as he could. He never begged for himself, but if someone happened to give him more than he needed, he gave it to someone in greater need. "He often begged on behalf of others," Father Groeschel notes, "and even organized the devout homeless into religious activities."

People in the neighborhood where he lived saw beneath the rags to the genuine love in this odd young man. When Benedict collapsed on the sidewalk in front of his favorite church and died, at the age of thirty-five, they raised the cry, "A saint is dead!"

CHRIST'S GRACE IS ENOUGH

Questions to Begin

15 minutes
Use a question or two to get warmed up for the reading.

1 When was the last time you deliberately did something that made you look silly?

2 When was the last time you *unconsciously* did something that made you look silly?

5 minutes
Read the passage aloud. Let individuals take turns reading paragraphs.

What's Happening

Paul has been put in a difficult position by those who criticize him for acting humbly. He has to defend himself. But it is hard to defend one's own humility, especially to those who do not find humility attractive. Paul does not want to boast about himself, because that would take the Corinthians' attention off the Lord—and, in any case, their idea of a Christian leader's cause for boasting is skewed. Yet Paul knows it will be helpful for them to see that he does not fall short even by their mistaken criteria for Christian leaders. He has to do *something* to show that the intruding missionaries are not nearly as impressive as they make themselves out to be. So Paul launches out into some boasting—foolishly, he admits. Yet Paul is clever enough to use his boasting—which turns out to be rather strange— to show the Corinthians that they need to adjust their thinking about Christian leadership and Christian life.

The Reading: 2 Corinthians 11:21–12:10

This Is Boasting?

11:21 But whatever anyone dares to boast of—I am speaking as a fool—I also dare to boast of that. 22 Are they Hebrews? So am I. Are they Israelites? So am I. Are they descendants of Abraham? So am I. 23 Are they ministers of Christ? I am talking like a madman—I am a better one: with far greater labors, far more imprisonments, with countless floggings, and often near death. 24 Five times I have received from the Jews the forty lashes minus one. 25 Three times I was beaten with rods. Once I received a stoning. Three times I was shipwrecked; for a night and a day I was adrift at sea; 26 on frequent journeys, in danger from rivers, danger from bandits, danger from my own people, danger from Gentiles, danger in the city, danger in the wilderness, danger at sea, danger from false brothers and sisters; 27 in toil and hardship, through many a sleepless night, hungry and thirsty, often without food, cold and naked. 28 And, besides other things, I am under daily pressure because of my anxiety for all the churches. 29 Who is weak, and I am not weak? Who is made to stumble, and I am not indignant?

30 If I must boast, I will boast of the things that show my weakness. 31 The God and Father of the Lord Jesus (blessed be he forever!) knows that I do not lie. 32 In Damascus, the governor under King Aretas guarded the city of Damascus in order to seize me, 33 but I was let down in a basket through a window in the wall, and escaped from his hands.

More Strange Boasting

12:1 It is necessary to boast; nothing is to be gained by it, but I will go on to visions and revelations of the Lord. 2 I know a person in Christ who fourteen years ago was caught up to the third heaven—whether in the body or out of the body I do not know; God knows. 3 And I know that such a person—whether in the body or out of the body I do not know; God knows— 4 was caught up into Paradise and heard things that are not to be told, that no mortal is permitted to repeat. 5 On behalf of such a one I will boast, but on my own behalf I will not boast, except of my weaknesses. 6 But if I wish to boast, I will not be a fool, for I will be speaking the truth. But I refrain from it, so that no one may think better of me than what is seen in me or heard from me, 7 even considering the exceptional character of the revelations.

Therefore, to keep me from being too elated, a thorn was given me in the flesh, a messenger of Satan to torment me, to keep me from being too elated. 8 Three times I appealed to the Lord about this, that it would leave me, 9 but he said to me, "My grace is sufficient for you, for power is made perfect in weakness." So, I will boast all the more gladly of my weaknesses, so that the power of Christ may dwell in me. 10 Therefore I am content with weaknesses, insults, hardships, persecutions, and calamities for the sake of Christ; for whenever I am weak, then I am strong.

10 minutes
Choose questions according to your interest and time.

1 Find all of Paul's statements to the effect that boasting is foolish. Why does he repeat this point?

2 From Paul's repeated scourgings by synagogue officials (11:24), what conclusion would you draw about his feelings toward his fellow Jews?

3 Referring to 12:8, someone might say to Paul, "God didn't answer your prayer." Would Paul agree?

4 A friend of yours has just read 11:23–27 and remarks that Paul was a masochist who liked pain. What would be your reply? Support your answer from what Paul says in this or earlier readings.

5 If a stoic's response to pain and hardship is "No big deal; I can handle it," is Paul a stoic?

6 What light does this reading shed on Paul's relationship with God? Cite specific verses to support your view.

A Guide to the Reading

*If participants have not read this section already, read it aloud.
Otherwise go on to "Questions for Application."*

11:21–33. Perhaps with wry humor, the sages who assembled the book of Proverbs put these maxims side by side: "Do not answer fools according to their folly, or you will be a fool yourself. Answer fools according to their folly, or they will be wise in their own eyes" (Proverbs 26:4–5). These contradictory proverbs express Paul's dilemma. "It is necessary to boast; nothing is to be gained by it, but I will go on. . . ." (12:1).

To judge from 11:21–22, the intruding missionaries have been boasting of their Jewishness to the mostly gentile Christians. Paul matches these boasts in 11:22. He is Jewish, born of Jewish parents, raised and educated as a Jew.

The intruders also apparently boast of their accomplishments as "ministers of Christ" (11:23). It seems that Paul is about to match their claims in this area too. "Are they ministers of Christ? . . . I am a better one" (11:23). We might expect Paul to continue with a list of achievements: I preached the gospel to thousands, founded Christian communities, converted opponents, protected the persecuted, and so on. But that is not the kind of list that Paul presents.

Paul declares that he has often been at the point of death (11:23) and indicates how. The kinds of scourgings and beatings he mentions (11:24–25) could be fatal. Stoning was a Jewish form of capital punishment. How did he survive it? Since the Romans probably did not allow Jewish communities to inflict capital punishment, the stoning he suffered was probably a spontaneous, poorly executed act by an angry mob (as in Acts 7:54–60; 14:19–20).

In addition to deadly dangers, Paul experiences tedious, low-grade suffering. "Toil and hardship" (11:27) probably refers to his long hours and difficult life as a poorly paid tent maker.

♦ "Through many a sleepless night"—perhaps he works nights in order to keep his days free for missionary work or works during the day and stays up at night to minister to workers who are free only after the end of the workday (see Acts 20).

♦ "Often without food"—either because he is too busy to sit down to a meal or because he lets his missionary work take him away from his workbench so much that he doesn't earn enough to buy his daily bread.

♦ "Cold and naked"—he can't afford decent clothing.

Who are the "weak" in 11:29: those without material resources? the sick? those with little faith? Whoever they are, Paul is in solidarity with them. There is a community of suffering among those who belong to Christ (Week 1), and Paul bears it in his heart.

Although Paul's catalogue of hardships demonstrates his courage and endurance, his purpose here is not to display his strength of character but to showcase his weaknesses and vulnerabilities. To make this point, he ends his list by mentioning a situation in which he looked ridiculous: being smuggled to safety disguised as a pile of laundry.

What exactly does Paul mean when he declares his wish to "boast of the things that show my weakness" (11:30)? Boasting usually means showing off a possession or accomplishment of which you are proud. How can someone be proud of their weaknesses? Boasting may also mean affirming that you base your confidence on something; for example, boasting about the Lord means declaring your certainty that the Lord will not let you down. But would it make any sense for a person to base their confidence on their weaknesses? Paul's meaning seems to be this: "I will gladly acknowledge the situations in which my weaknesses are exposed, because those situations give me the opportunity to trust God and experience God's power."

At 11:23, Paul seemed about to show that he surpasses the intruding missionaries in areas in which they boast. But instead he has described the kinds of experiences that the intruders probably would not boast about, that is, experiences that expose his weaknesses. The other missionaries are domineering and exploitative (11:20). If they *had* experienced the kinds of hardships that Paul has suffered, they would probably not publicize them. Stories about their being publicly beaten, thrown into jail, and forced to wear ragged clothes would damage their image as powerful, successful, inspiring evangelists.

Paul's strange bragging about his inability to protect himself from hardship and pain challenges the Corinthians to reconsider what is worth boasting about. What is admirable? Having great successes? displaying impressive talents? being a celebrity? following Jesus through thick and thin?

12:1–7. Perhaps the intruding missionaries are also talking proudly about spiritual revelations they have received. Here, too, Paul starts off in a way that leads us to expect that he will beat the other missionaries at their own game. But again, he does so in a way that implicitly rejects the rules of the game.

Paul tells of an amazing spiritual experience. He was lifted up to "the third heaven," or "Paradise"—probably terms for the same heavenly realm. But he distances himself from the vision: he refers to himself as "a person" (12:2) and says that while he will show off what "such a one" experienced, he will not boast about it himself (12:5). This is Paul's way of keeping his private spiritual experience separate from his public role as an apostle. The intruders are apparently citing their revelatory experiences as evidence of their qualification for leadership. Paul disagrees with this criterion. He too has had such experiences, but he does not regard them as relevant for establishing apostolic credentials. Whether or not a person has vivid spiritual experiences is irrelevant to his or her being qualified for leadership in the Church.

Paul is oddly uncommunicative about his vision. He emphasizes that he doesn't know how he experienced it (12:2–3), and he declines to describe what he saw or heard. He seems to be making fun of the intruders. They have challenged him to a competition to see whose spiritual revelation is greatest. His entry into the competition is a complete blank: an experience that cannot be described, a revelation that cannot be revealed. It is like entering an invisible dog in the American Kennel Club competition for Best In Show.

12:7–10. In Paul's view, spiritual experiences carry a risk. They can pump up the receiver's self-image, producing an inflated sense of his or her holiness. To prick this dangerous balloon, Paul reports, God gave him a "thorn . . . in the flesh." The Greek could also be translated "a thorn *for* the flesh," in other words, a painful problem designed to keep the flesh—Paul's pride—from overinflation. There is no way to know what the thorn was, because Paul does not tell us. It could have been a chronic illness. In any case, it was a distressing weakness.

Significantly, Paul did not find it easy to accept his thorn. He prayed repeatedly for the problem to be removed. Only after some time did he submit to God's wish that he continue to experience this weakness. Clearly, like us, Paul went through a process of learning that weaknesses and pains are an opportunity for trusting God and experiencing his power.

Again, Paul says he will "boast" of his weaknesses (also 11:30). Notice that Paul not only *describes* his weaknesses but *boasts* about them. He realizes that our weaknesses are the realm in which Christ's power becomes present in us—if we acknowledge and accept them as part of God's plan for us. It is not weakness alone but weakness accepted with faith that opens us to God's power.

Reflections. Paul boasts of his weaknesses in order to counter the values that the intruding missionaries are promoting. In Paul's view, what is important for Christian leadership is whether you love and serve people, despite your weaknesses and suffering, not whether you have extraordinary talents or amazing spiritual experiences. What makes a Christian leader—what makes a Christian—is joining Jesus in his experience of being "crucified in weakness" and being made alive "by the power of God" (13:4). The cross was where God worked through Jesus for the salvation of the world. Our sharing in Jesus' cross is where God works in and through us. This is a liberating truth, although sometimes almost intolerably hard.

God sent Paul on a mission. As Paul went on his assignment, his weaknesses were glaringly exposed. He had no wealth to provide for his needs, so he suffered hunger and cold. He had no personal security crew to protect him, so he was beaten in synagogues. He had no expensive lawyers to defend him, so he was beaten by municipal officials. He had to cross the sea and so was vulnerable to shipwreck; he had to travel through the countryside and so was exposed to bandits. Paul was constantly moving outside his comfort zone, to say the least. If he had stayed home, he could have avoided suffering at least some of his weaknesses, but he went on with his mission.

Paul's calling is different from ours. But the pattern we see in his life is the pattern for us too. As we go on the path where Christ leads us, our weaknesses are exposed. Then, if we are willing, Christ's power will become active in us.

Questions for Application

40 minutes
Choose questions according to your interest and time.

1 From this reading, what would you say is Paul's view of success and failure in life? Are there differences between your view and his?

2 Reflect on the way you have seen the same kind of suffering affect people differently: some grow spiritually, some become angry and bitter. What accounts for the difference?

3 From Paul's experience of prayer in 12:8–10, what can you learn for your own relationship with Christ?

4 Paul could have gained stature in other people's eyes by highlighting his experiences of mystical prayer, but he didn't. By what criteria did he want others to evaluate him? Are you sometimes inclined to boost yourself in others' estimation? What could you learn from Paul?

5 Paul was in solidarity with the weak. With what weak person is God calling you to be in solidarity this week? How can you show it?

6   For personal reflection: What
    personal weaknesses are you
    most aware of right now? How
    would these areas of your life
    look if you viewed them with
    trust in God? How might God
    use these areas of your life as
    opportunities to show you—and
    others—his love?

7   For personal reflection: People
    are commonly hesitant to let
    others see their weaknesses.
    Are you? Why? What are the
    dangers and opportunities
    in letting others see your
    weaknesses, failings, or
    suffering? What can you learn
    from Paul's boasting about his
    weaknesses?

8   How has 2 Corinthians helped
    you to understand God's power
    in human weakness? What
    action will you take in response
    to what you have learned?

Approach to Prayer

15 minutes
Use this approach—or create your own!

♦ Pray this litany to St. Paul aloud, pausing after each sentence. Between sentences, let the other participants pray the refrain "St. Paul, pray for us."

St. Paul, you trusted in the Father of mercies and God of all consolation.

You taught us to set our hope in God and never lose heart.

You proclaimed Jesus Christ as Lord, in good times and in bad.

You set us an example of walking by faith, not by sight.

You pointed us toward the coming kingdom and our transformation from one degree of glory to another.

God's power was made perfect in your weakness.

Conclude by praying the following aloud:

O God, who have taught the whole world by the preaching of blessed Paul the Apostle, grant that we who celebrate his memory may, by following his example, be drawn to you, through our Lord Jesus Christ, your Son, who lives and reigns with you in the unity of the Holy Spirit, forever and ever. Amen.

Saints in the Making

An Experience of God's Power

This section is a supplement for individual reading.

By an anonymous Bible reader

I had a very bad temper—at work, with my wife, and with my children. I used to be a five-temper-a-week man. That is, I would lose my temper about five times a week.

In the past few months, I hardly ever lose my temper. Even when I do, it does not consume me. It is not because my children have grown up and moved on. It's not because my marriage has matured. It's not because my workplace has improved. I believe it is because of the healing power of Jesus.

For years, my spirit was willing but my flesh was weak. I could not handle things when they did not go my way. I would lose my temper. Afterward, I would say to myself, "Why did you act so childish? Was it really that big a deal?" I would feel guilty. Often, I would get into a mood. Each time, I would resolve to control my temper. I would start off okay, but then it would happen—a situation would arise and I would lose my temper.

In my prayer time, I was reading the Scriptures. Paul's words jumped out at me: "My grace is sufficient for you, for power is made perfect in weakness" (2 Corinthians 12:9). Suddenly, it dawned on me that God's grace, not my willpower, was going to be the way to control my temper.

Now, I pray each day: "Jesus, I am weak and you are strong. I have a bad temper. Help me. Your grace is sufficient for me. I do not want this temper. I give it over to you. Please, Jesus, deal directly with my temper. I will not submit to this temper any longer." I began to see my temper lessen. It was truly amazing. Things that used to cause me to fly off the handle now could not cause my temper to flair. Even when I do lose my temper (I am not perfect yet), it is not nearly as dominating as it used to be. I catch myself, I stop, and I pray, "Your grace is sufficient." I think I am more able to control my temper as each day passes.

In the next verse, Paul writes, "Therefore I am content with weaknesses, . . . for the sake of Christ; for whenever I am weak, then I am strong" (2 Corinthians 12:10). I tried to control my temper on my own. I could not. When I called on the power of God, I found a power to help me find peace.

Suggestions for Bible Discussion Groups

L ike a camping trip, a Bible discussion group works best if you agree on where you're going and how you intend to get there. Many groups use their first meeting to talk over such questions. Here is a checklist of issues, with bits of advice from people who have experience in Bible discussions. (A planning discussion will go more smoothly if the leaders have thought through the following issues beforehand.)

Agree on your purpose. Are you getting together to gain wisdom and direction for your lives? to finally get acquainted with the Bible? to support one another in following Christ? to encourage those who are exploring—or reexploring—the Church? for other reasons?

Agree on attitudes. For example: "We're all beginners here." "We're here to help one another understand and respond to God's word." "We're not here to offer counseling or direction to one another." "We want to read Scripture prayerfully." What do *you* wish to emphasize? Make it explicit!

Agree on ground rules. Barbara J. Fleischer, in her useful book *Facilitating for Growth,* recommends that a group clearly state its approach to the following:

- *Preparation.* Do we agree to read the material and prepare answers to the questions before each meeting?
- *Attendance.* What kind of priority will we give to our meetings?
- *Self-revelation.* Are we willing to help the others in the group gradually get to know us—our weaknesses as well as our strengths, our needs as well as our gifts?
- *Listening.* Will we commit ourselves to listen to one another?
- *Confidentiality.* Will we keep everything that is shared *with* the group *in* the group?
- *Discretion.* Will we refrain from sharing about the faults and sins of people who are not in the group?
- *Encouragement and support.* Will we give as well as receive?
- *Participation.* Will we give each person the time and opportunity to make a contribution?

You could probably take a pen and draw a circle around *listening* and *confidentiality.* Those two points are especially important.

The following items could be added to Fleischer's list:

♦ *Relationship with parish.* Is our group part of the adult faith-formation program? independent but operating with the express approval of the pastor? not a parish-based group?

♦ *New members.* Will we let new members join us once we have begun the six weeks of discussions?

Agree on housekeeping.

♦ *When will we meet?*

♦ *How often will we meet?* Meeting weekly or every other week is best if you can manage it. William Riley remarks, "Meetings once a month are too distant from each other for the threads of the last session not to be lost" (*The Bible Study Group: An Owner's Manual*).

♦ *How long will each meeting run?*

♦ *Where will we meet?*

♦ *Is any setup needed?* Christine Dodd writes that "the problem with meeting in a place like a church hall is that it can be very soul-destroying," given the cold, impersonal feel of many church facilities. If you have to meet in a church facility, Dodd recommends doing something to make the area homey (*Making Scripture Work*).

♦ *Who will host the meetings?* Leaders and hosts are not necessarily the same people.

♦ *Will we have refreshments?* Who will provide them? Don Cousins and Judson Poling make this recommendation: "Serve refreshments if you like, but save snacks and other foods for the end of the meeting to minimize distractions" (*Leader's Guide 1*).

♦ *What about child care?* Most experienced leaders of Bible discussion groups discourage bringing infants or other children to adult Bible discussions.

Agree on leadership. You need someone to facilitate—to keep the discussion on track, to see that everyone has a chance to speak, to help the group stay on schedule. Rena Duff, editor of the newsletter *Sharing God's Word Today,* recommends having two or three people take turns leading the discussions.

It's okay if the leader is not an expert on the Bible. You have this Six Weeks book as a guide, and if questions come up that no one can answer, you can delegate a participant to do a little research between meetings. Perhaps your parish priest or someone on the pastoral staff of your parish could offer advice. Or help may be available from your diocesan catechetical office or a local Catholic college or seminary.

It's important for the leader to set an example of listening, to draw out the quieter members (and occasionally restrain the more vocal ones), to move the group on when it gets stuck, to get the group back on track when the discussion moves away from the topic, and to restate and summarize what the group is learning. Sometimes the leader needs to remind the members of their agreements. An effective group leader is enthusiastic about the topic and the discussions and sets an example of learning from others and of using resources for growing in understanding.

As a discussion group matures, other members of the group will increasingly share in doing all these things on their own initiative.

Bible discussion is an opportunity to experience the fulfillment of Jesus' promise "Where two or three are gathered in my name, I am there among them" (Matthew 18:20). Put your discussion group in Jesus' hands. Pray for the guidance of the Spirit. And have a great time exploring God's word together!

Suggestions for Individuals

Y ou can use this book just as well for individual study as for group discussion. While discussing the Bible with other people can be a rich experience, there are advantages to reading on your own. For example:

♦ You can focus on the points that interest you most.

♦ You can go at your own pace.

♦ You can be completely relaxed and unashamedly honest in your answers to all the questions, since you don't have to share them with anyone!

My suggestions for using this book on your own are these:

♦ Don't skip "Questions to Begin." The questions can help you as an individual reader warm up to the topic of the reading.

♦ Take your time on "Questions for Careful Reading" and "Questions for Application." While a group will probably not have enough time to work on all the questions, you can allow yourself the time to consider all of them if you are using the book by yourself.

♦ After reading "Guide to the Reading," go back and reread the Scripture text before answering the Questions for Application.

♦ Take the time to look up all the parenthetical Scripture references in the introduction, the Guides to the Reading, and the other material.

♦ Since you control the pace, give yourself plenty of opportunities to reflect on the meaning of the Scripture passages for you. Let your reading be an opportunity for these words to become God's words to you.

Resources

Bibles

The following editions of the Bible contain the full set of biblical books recognized by the Catholic Church, along with a great deal of useful explanatory material:
- The Catholic Study Bible (Oxford University Press), which uses the text of the New American Bible
- The Catholic Bible: Personal Study Edition (Oxford University Press), which also uses the text of the New American Bible
- The New Jerusalem Bible, the regular (not the reader's) edition (Doubleday)

Books, Web Sites, and Other Resources

- C. K. Barrett, *The Second Epistle to the Corinthians* (Peabody, MA: Hendrickson Publishers, 1993).
- Frank J. Matera, *II Corinthians* (Louisville: Westminster John Knox Press, 2003).

How has Scripture had an impact on your life? Was this book helpful to you in your study of the Bible? Please send comments, suggestions, and personal experiences to Kevin Perrotta, General Editor, Editorial Department, Loyola Press, 3441 N. Ashland Ave., Chicago, IL 60657.